“KAYASTH KUL NIRNAY”

Khoob Chand's Urdu Book entitled

"KAYASTH KUL NIRNAY"

(Determination of Kayasth Community)

Select Genealogies of Renowned Kayasths

Edited, Updated and Translated
Into English

By

Dr Narayan Raj

GYAN

The Publication of this Book has been financially supported by the Indian Council of Historical Research (ICHR). The responsibility for the Facts Stated or Opinions Expressed is Entirely of the Author and not of the Council.

First Published, 2018

Published by

Gyan Publishing House
5, Ansari Road
Daryaganj, New Delhi-110002
Phone: 9811692060
E-mail: books@gyanbooks.com

Printed at: G. Print Process, Delhi.

Cataloging in Publication Data—DK
Courtesy: D.K. Agencies (P) Ltd. <docinfo@dkagencies.com>

Khoob Chand, active 19th century, **author.**
Khoob Chand's Urdu book entitled "Kayasth kul Nirnay" = Determination of Kayasth community: select genealogies of renowned Kayasths / edited, updated and translated by Dr Narayan Raj.
pages cm
ISBN 9788121214087 (hardback)

1. Kayasthas—History. 2. Kayasthas—India—Genealogy. 3. India—Genealogy. I. Nārāin Rāj, editor, translator. II. Title. III. Title: Determination of Kayasth community.

DS432.K29C43 2017 DDC 929.072054 23

DEDICATED

To

Well known Kayasths

Swami Vivekananda

Sri Aurobindo Ghosh

And

Netaji Subhash Chandra Bose

Contents

PART - II

Preface

As per the Hindu scriptures, Kayasths are the descendants of Sri Chitraguptji who appeared from the entire body of Lord Brahma (this has been dealt with in detail in this book). Sri Chitraguptji is responsible to record the deeds of human beings. He had twelve children from his two wives i.e. Shobhavati and Kumudini (This has also been dealt with in this book in detail).

Kayasths are Kshatriyas by caste. In the early period, Kayasthas were kings and rulers in different parts of India. They were responsible for writing documents, maintaining records and accounts since seventh century.

Kayasths served in various capacities right from Prime Minister of a country to a treasury official. During the thirteenth century, when the Hindu kings were ruling India, Kayasths were holding very high positions in government. When the Guptas were the rulers, they sought the help of Kayasths to manage the administration of the state.

The fact cannot be denied that Kayasths played an important role in administration of the state during different periods. They moulded themselves according to the requirements of their masters or the rulers. For instance, during the Mughal rule in India, they mastered themselves in Persian language which was the official language of Mughal Court.

Raja Todarmal, who was a Kayasth and the Minister during Akbar's period, was one among the *Navratnas* of Akbar. He was a linguist who translated *Bhagwat Purana* from Sanskrit into Persian.

As a result of their proximity to the rulers, many Kayasths became *Zamindars* as well. Some of them became Governors and Treasury officials, during Mughal rule.

Kayasths were holding prominent positions during British Raj also. They were not only administrators but served in finance and judiciary also.

India, before independence, had more than 600 princely states. Kayasths occupied prominent positions in most of these states. Their closeness to the rulers testifies to the fact that they enjoyed the confidence of the rulers. In some of the states, they were *Diwans* i.e. Prime Ministers and Ministers. The Nizam of Hyderabad entrusted the entire Revenue Department under the control of the family of Raja Shiv Raj Dharamwanth Bahadur who was a Kayasth. The royal kitchen of the Nizam was under the supervision of Raja Girdhari Pershad alias Bansi Raja who was also a Kayasth. This is indicative of the fact that the Nizam of Hyderabad had great trust in Kayasth Community.

Kayasths played an important role during the pre-independence era in the Independent Movement of India. Some of the notable Kayasths are: Swami Vivekananda, Sri Aurobindo Ghosh, Netaji Subhash Chandra Bose, Dr Rajendra Prasad, Lal Bahadur Shastri, Jai Prakash Narayan, Munshi Prem Chand, Maha Devi Varma, Dr Shanti Swaroop Bhatnagar. It was my earnest desire to write especially about Swami Vivekananda, Netaji Subhash Chandra Bose and others, but due to my ill health and paucity of time, I could not do so. I hope that in future, some Kayasth will write about them.

It is an established fact that Kayasths are peace-loving community and they never indulged in any unnecessary disputes.

The fact cannot be ignored that Kayasths are scholars of repute in Sanskrit, Hindi, Persian, Urdu and in many other languages. Many of them are poets of these languages.

The old doctrine that Kayasths were better suited for pen rather than sword was proved by the literary merits of the Kayasths like Munshi Prem Chand, Maha Devi Varma, Ram Babu Saxena (the author of "The History of Urdu Literature") and many others.

The rarest of the rare is the family of Raja Girdhari Pershad alias Bansi Raja of Hyderabad, a Kayasth of Saxena family, whose seven generations were authors and writers in six languages i.e. Persian, Urdu, Hindi, Braj Bhasha, Awadhi and English.

Today, in India, Kayasths are holding key positions. They are in politics and administration in the Central Government. They are very senior bureaucrats, doctors, lawyers, scientists and professionals in different disciplines.

I was fortunate to lay hands on a book entitled "Kayasth Kul Nirnay" which was compiled in Urdu by Khoobchand, a Kayasth Srivastav of Banaras city which was published in Hyderabad in 1892.

On going through this book, two things impressed me most:

Firstly, it gives the details about Lord Brahmaji and Sri Chitraguptji. Besides this, it also gives valuable information about the Universe.

Secondly, it gives the genealogy or the family trees of about fifty Kayasth families. This is a rare and valuable piece of information.

'Kayasth Kul Nirnay' was originally written in Urdu. It was published in 1892 at Aftaab-e-Deccan Press, Hyderabad. I, therefore, decided to translate it into English for the benefit of large number of Non-Urdu reading generations.

Translating it from Urdu into English was a formidable task, specially the names of persons and places. In case, there is any spelling mistake in the names, I sincerely apologize. I am glad that the work is completed after overcoming many hurdles.

I have taken liberty to edit, update and give additional information wherever possible in the original text.

After completing this Herculean task, I decided to include a short biography of some of the leading Kayasth personalities. I selected two freedom fighters, two literary personalities and one scientist. They are: Dr Rajendra Prasad, Lal Bahadur Shastri, Munshi Prem Chand, Maha Devi Varma and Dr Shanti Swaroop Bhatnagar. There are many other distinguished Kayasth personalities who could not be included for paucity of time and my ill health. I also edited and updated the write-ups of some of the Kayasth families from the original texts, such as, the family of Raja Girdhari Pershad alias Bansi Raja, Raja Shiv Raj Dharamwanth, Rai Murlidhar etc. but could not do all that I wanted due to lack of communication and non-availability of material with the respective families. This additional information has been mentioned under the sub-heading **"Also See",** in Part-I of the book.

In short, it can be concluded that Kayasths played a prominent role during all the periods of Indian History, especially in politics, administration, finance etc.

Two of the Kayasths were awarded the highest civilian award "Bharat Ratna" by Government of India. They are: Dr Rajendra Prasad and Lal Bahadur Shastri.

Dr Rajendra Prasad, a Kayasth was the first President of the Republic of India for a decade and Sri Lal Bahadur Shastri, another Kayasth was the Prime Minister of India for a short period. He passed away while he was Prime Minister.

I am highly indebted to Mr Syed Rafiuddin Quadri, son of Dr Syed Mohiuddin Quadri Zore for his guidance and help in my work. His interest in the progress of my work acted as a stimulant for me, which I often needed and cherished. On several occasions, he inspired me with his valuable advice. Without his unstinted support, my task would not have been accomplished. I appreciate the deep understanding, co-operation, perceptiveness, enthusiasm, endurance; inspiration and constant support which he offered me to complete this work.

I am grateful to Professor Syed Khaja Moinuddin of the Department of Translation of Maulana Azad National Urdu University, Hyderabad, for his unstinted help in the translation of the book **"Kayasth Kul Nirnay"** from Urdu into English. Without his help this task would not have been completed. He continued to evince keen interest in my work for which he merits great appreciation. He generously shared his views on translation work. I owe much to him. I am also thankful to him for going through the manuscript of the book meticulously.

I appreciate the support of Dr Mohd. Ziauddin Ahmed Shakeb (London) from time to time.

I am thankful to Sri Jeevan Raj Saxena for his help in composing and collating the text of this book.

Finally, I am extremely grateful to the Indian Council of Historical Research, New Delhi, for its financial assistance in meeting the production cost.

Dr Narayan Raj

PART-I

English Translation of

Khoob Chand's Urdu Book entitled

"Kayasth Kul Nirnay"

(Determination of Kayasth Community)

Select Genealogies of Renowned Kayasths

By

Dr. Narayan Raj

English Translation of the Title Page of the original Urdu Book

Sar sabz rahe daher mein bagh-e-Asaf,
Mahbub Ali Shah Chirag-e-Asaf

[Let the garden of Asaf remain green in the world,
Mahboob Ali, the King, is the lamp of Asaf].

KAYASTH KUL NIRNAY

[Determination of the Kayasth Community]

It was compiled by Khoob Chand a Kayasth of Srivastav caste, Second Munshi (Clerk) of the territory of Palmer Sahab Bahadur, resident of Prahalad Ghat, Banaras City, presently residing at Chaderghat, Hyderabad Deccan.

Munshi Gahwarleet Lal, another Kayasth of Srivastav caste and other residents of *Bastiyan* of Jonepur District presently residing at locality Kabeer Chowraha, Banaras city.

Shri Ganesh

After reciting it to Gauri Putra (son of Parvati meaning Ganesh) I will ask for the fulfillment of my desire.

Remove obstacle and make me happy. I implead with folded hands to bless me to make this book novel or unique.

Horoscope

O' God! Listen to my hope and fulfill it. You are the greatest of all Shastras and Puranas. Say that you are the greatest of all Gods, Goddesses, Pandits and wisemen, all of you listen.

Oh God! expand the heart of Khoob Chand. Spread this light.

This is my hope.

Introduction

This devotee, Khoob Chand, is the resident of the city of Banaras in the locality of Prahalad Ghat, caste Kayasth, Srivastav, progeny of Pandiya. This city is now called 'Dildar Nagar'. I have been staying in this city for the past 45 years. I have been in the clerical service of Mr Thomas Palmer Sahab Bahadur, Councilor for the past 33 years. I travelled with him to the Northern and the Western areas including Bengal. For the past seven years, I have been staying with him in Hyderabad Deccan. He is very gracious and helpful to the poor. He helps the destitute. His attributes are beyond description. For the past 45 years, he has been taking care of 20 of his servants and relatives. May God continue his patronage.

Incidentally, on one day, I was immersed in the river of thoughts in the state of inactivity. My son, Ganesh Pershad asked me "what it is that you are thinking?" I told him that due to inactivity, I am thinking what to do? He then told me that he does not know very well the names of his relatives and the details of their families, so far. During this period of inactivity, you may please write a book for our awareness and commemoration in which the details of the family members are mentioned so that we should know about them properly. On the insistence of my son, my heart consented to take myself out of this river of inactivity. It occurred to me that if I write the details of only my family and my relatives, other persons of our community would pay little attention to it. On account of this thought, I proposed to write the details of the genesis of Sri Brahmaji Maharaj and the mundane Universe, the emergence of Sri Chitraguptji Maharaj who is the progenitor, right from his birth and also the members of Kayasth caste with the determination of their sects hierarchically. For this purpose,

I started writing letters to other relatives for getting the details of their family trees. Some persons sent these details in two or four months and some of them kept quiet. The replies of many other persons are still awaited. I wanted to write the details on the basis of the letters received so far. Incidentally, during this period, Gahwarleet Lal Sahab, a rich nobleman of Zafarabad, Jonepur District, presently residing at Karchone locality of Banaras city, Attorney and Munshi of Maharaja Som Sekhara Chandra, Minister of Raja Korak, who is also one of our relatives came to Hyderabad with Maharaja Sahab.

On one day, I was sitting engrossed in the above mentioned thoughts, Munshi Sahab came and asked me, "what is that you are worrying about?" I showed the draft of this book and told him that for the past so many years, I have been corresponding with the relatives to send the details of their families together with their family trees, some of them sent them. On hearing this, Munshi Sahab told me that "if you continue to wait in this manner, it would take a lot of time and you know it very well that your borrowed impermanent life is not trustworthy. There is no certainty of your life. Make haste to the extent possible." I then told Munshi Sahab, if he helps me, it is possible to accomplish this task early. He readily accepted it and helped me a lot. On my insistence, he got the details of his family and his relatives together with their family trees. He went through the draft of my book and rectified it chronologically. Due to his attention, this task could be accomplished successfully. I, therefore, named this book as "Kayasth Kul Nirnay" (Determination of Kayasth Community) and divided it into five chapters.

Chapter–I consists of description of Brahmaji's progeny, family tree and the creation of Universe.

Chapter–II consists of the birth of Sri Chitraguptji with the progeny and determination of their sects (Verna) together with the precedents of the court and the proofs of the previous Pandits of Kashi, Kashmir, Pune and Nadiad etc.

Chapter–III consists of practices and duties of the caste of Kayasths together with their lineages and the method of worshipping Sri Chitraguptji Maharaj.

Chapter–IV contains family tree of self, relatives and others.

Chapter-V contains the description of members of family, brief description of Srivastav, Mathur, Saxena, Asthana and other brethren of the community in the City of Hyderabad Deccan.

Khoob Chand

31st December 1892

Chapter – I

Description of the Progeny of Sri Brahmaji and the Creation of the Universe

It is depicted in the Sri Rig Veda that before the creation of the Universe, there was darkness and water everywhere completely. It can't be described.

For the manifestation of *Parameshwar* into the world, a square platform of twenty four trunks of trees was prepared. It has been mentioned in *Shikhar Shastra.* He accepted this and made his appearance in Universal form in which the entire creation is manifested. He created Brahmaji from the stalk of a lotus flower but Brahmaji did not know who created him, who is he and where has he come from? In this incantation, 100 heads used to get into the stalk of the lotus and come out of it.

On one occasion sitting on the stalk of the lotus flower, Brahmaji started looking here and there. Suddenly, Brahmaji got four heads. Brahmaji then, looked upwards. He heard a noise from the sky "tup, tup, tup" the meaning of "tup" is to worship and chit means lying ventrally. It means to think of *Parameshwar.* Brahmaji worshipped for one thousand years. Then, *Parameshwar* assumed the shape of Chitrabhoj and gave his appearance (*Darshan*) and told Brahmaji to create *Shrishti* (Creatures). Brahmaji asked him how to create. At that time, *Parameshwar* showed him *Chitra Slok Bhagwat* and told him that this *Ashlok* is in the 9th chapter of the 2nd part of the Bhagwat. Then, Brahmaji thought of creating creatures (*Shrishti*) but everywhere there was water, so he could not create anything. With the blessings of *Parameshwar,* he drank entire water, then from the same twenty four trunks of the trees which Eshwar had created earlier, he created Heaven (*Swarg*) and Earth (*Prithivi*) and in between the two, he created Sky etc. and created four sons (1) Satak, (2) Vasnandan, (3) Vasant Kumar and (4) Sanatan. When he inclined towards creation, he created ten (10) more sons from whom the entire creatures (*Shrishti*) were created. This fact would be known from the progeny or the family tree of Brahmaji, which is entered in this book. At that time, Brahmaji created Brahman from his mouth, Kshatri from Vibhoja, Vaishya (Trader) from Dadro and Shudra (now they are referred to as Dalits) from feet and popularized the same names as four sects (*Varan*). These names are entered in the family tree of Brahmaji but when he started to review the status (*Hasab*) of their religion (*Dharma*) or non-religion (*Adharma*), then in his view nobody could measure upto his standard. Brahmaji then, sat for offering worship (*Tapasya*). After a long time, from his powers, he created Baba Chitraguptji Maharaj and founded the new community of the Kayasths in Kshatri sect. Its authenticity is mentioned in detail in this book.

Creation of Brahmaand: When Brahmaji completed the creation of the primary or the first Creation (*Shrishti*), he created four periods (*Yug*) which are: *Satyug (Satjug), Treta, Dwapar and Kalyug.*

For the delight of all, he made Shamboo Manoon king. In this manner, fourteen Manoons became Kings and every Manoon ruled for seventy-one *Chowkdi* and they are still ruling. Four *Yugs* (Periods) constitute one *chowkdi,* then it is one day of Brahmaji. When a day's work of Brahmaji gets finished, he then, sleeps. *Nanditon Lok* means: *Lok Patal, Lok Varg, Lok Kaparlay* which is called *Avantar Parlay.*

After it, Brahmaji starts creating the world. (*Shrishti Ki Rachna*) and takes one *manu*. When fourteen Manoons finished their rule, then it is equal to one day and one night of Brahmaji. In this manner, when hundred years of Brahmaji get spent, then he sleeps. Then, it will be *Parlay* of all the three Lok (Universe) i.e. Bhoo Lok, Paataal Lok and Swarg Lok. It is called *Maha Parlay*, during this period *(Parlay),* no one survives. In *Satjug*, one king spent the *yug* (period). During this period, King Bain was born to his queen and he became *Maha Vishisht.* He told his father and all the subjects (people) that "I am *Eeshwar* and all of you should worship me alone". Whosoever violated his order, he used to kill him.

At that time, Brahmins saw that this Vashisht had started troubling everyone. Brahmins then, cursed him and burnt him to ashes. When there was no king, on the Earth, first his father went for offering prayers then, Brahmins did the reconstruction (*Jangamantham*) of Raja Bain which resulted in the creation of an ugly black man. Brahmins named him Kol Bahel and assigned him the rule of mountainous land *(Pahadi Zameen)*. Brahmins then performed *Bhojamantham.* Then, Raja Partho Maha Tejwant emerged from it. After assigning the role of the entire Earth (*Prithvi*) Brahmins engaged themselves in their religious activities. Raja Partho, son of Raja Bain went to forest one day for hunting. He saw that the land has ups and downs and by covering with mountains, the residents of the village get ruined. Due to the cruelty of Raja Bain, seeds were not shooting forth from the Earth and nothing was growing. Due to this, the people used to die of starvation. People then made a representation to Raja Partho that they are dying of hunger. On hearing this, Raja Partho got angry with the land. He took the bow and arrow and went to shoot it. Vexed up with this, the Earth ran away changing its form. When Khain Saran did not see, then the Earth came to Raja Partho. The Earth folded her arms and told "O Maharaj? Why do you beat me." Raja told that why doesn't she produce foodgrains for the people. It replied that it does not produce food grains due to the cruelty of Raja Bain. The Earth told that it would show a trick and asked him to milk-pain, that is, extract milk from it. Raja then, called the subjects and the Gods. Raja himself assumed the guise of a calf ploughed the soil along with the subjects and Gods extracted food grains and vegetation from the Earth.

From among the Gods of Indradesa, Brahspatji assumed the shape of a calf. He produced *Amrut* from the cow. All the Gods took milk in golden pots. Then, Raja Partho fondled his hands on the cow and asked it to say if it had any grief. The Earth then, told "Maharaj"! I get pained when I am covered with mountains. Telling this, the cow disappeared. Raja stripped off the feathers of the mountains and leveled the Earth straight, determined the distance in *Kos* (nearly four miles) and later inhabited the villages and cities.

Creation of Oceans and Islands

Raja Sambhutatvo assigned the governance of the Earth to his son, Raja Priya Brat and went for offering prayers *(Tapasya)*. Then, Narad came and told Priya Brat that this world is very small and asked him to worship *(Tapasya)*. He became ascetic *(Sanyasi)* and went to the temple of Badrinathji and sat at the mountain of Konda Marli Parbat. Brahmaji saw that the world is free from king and there must be someone to administer it. Then Brahmaji and Shambumanu came to Priya Brat and asked him, "O son! why did you abandon governance?" He did not care for his words. Brahmaji made him understand that getting involved in the household affairs; he should worship *Eeshwar* and administer the Earth. Wisdom dawned on Priya Brat and he started ruling. Brahmaji and Shambumanu went to their places. King Priya Brat ruled for eleven Arab years. (100 crore make one Arab).

One day, Suraj Narayan (Sun) did not rise. Priya Brat thought that there should be no night. It should always be day. Raja Priya Brat boarded the chariot and went to catch the Sun. He ran for seven tait to catch Surya Narayan but he could not get him. Brahmaji made him understand that the Sun is the art of *Eeshwar*. After hearing this conversation, he came back. Out of the wheel of his chariot, seven islands and seven oceans were formed, according to the following details:

Details of Islands and Oceans as Mentioned in Veda and Shastra.

Details of the Islands:

Length and breadth of the Jumbo Island- *Lakh Jojan.*

Length and breadth of Salbali Island – Double of Jumbo Island.

Length and breadth of Koonch Island – Double of Salbali Island.

Length and breadth of Pushkar Island – Double of Koonch Island.

Length and breadth of Parlokya Island – Double of Pushkar Island.

Length and breadth of Kas Island – Double of Parlokya Island.

Length and breadth of Naag Island- Double of Kas Island.

Details of Oceans

Length and breadth of Khaar Ocean – *Lakh Jojan* long and wide.

Length and breath of Akso Ocean – Double of Khaar Ocean.

Length and breadth of Dohi Ocean – Double of Akso Ocean

Length and breadth of Madhu Ocean – Double of Dohi Ocean.

Length and breadth of Mudra Ocean – Double of Madhu Ocean.

Length and breadth of Sidha Odak Ocean – Double of Mudra Ocean.

Length and breadth of Kesar Ocean – Double of Sidha Ocean.

THIS IS THE MAP

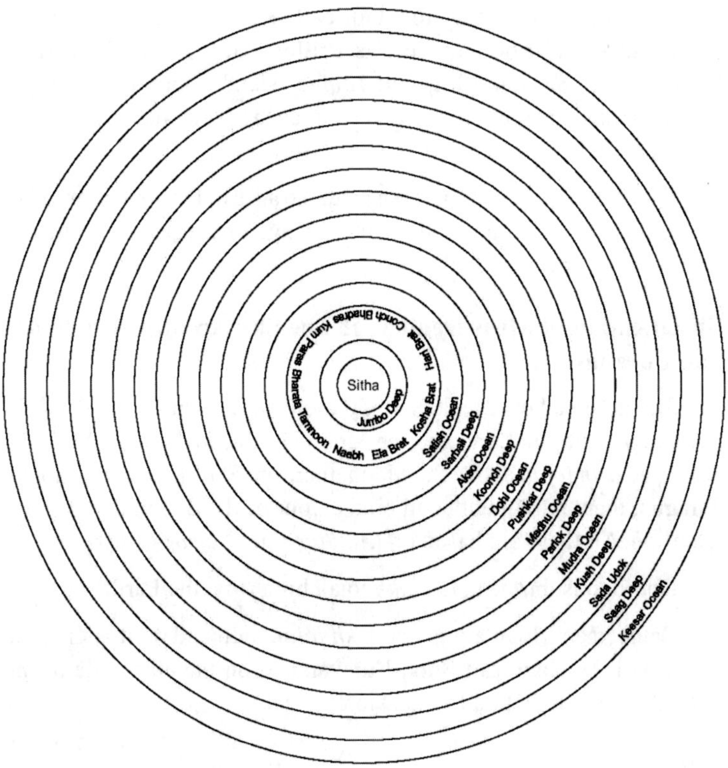

It may be noted that there are nine *Khands* (Portions) in Jumbo Dweep (Island). It is made by Raja Naabh

(1) Naabh (2) Ela Brat (3) Kusa Brat (4) Hari Brat
(5) Cronch (6) Bhadras (7) Kampras (8) Bharata
(9) Tamnoon – non-barar

It may be noted that in Jumbo Island, there are nine *Khands.*

It was constructed by Raja Naabh.

1. Naabh, 2. Ela Brat, 3. Kusa Brat, 4. Hari Brat, 5. Cronch, 6. Bhadras, 7. Kampras, 8. Bharata, 9. Tamnoon non-barar.

In Jojan, there is one *Khand* (Tank) each and in Islands, there are seven *Khands* (tanks) but the largest of all is, Bharata Khand. The entire Earth *(Pruthvi)* is fifty crore Jojan.

After this, there is a mountain called "Lokaloki" and the Sun is behind it and after it, there is Prithvi Kunjan and Sambargar Mountain is *lakh jojan* high. In Jumbo Island, there are 27 major mountains and in other islands, there are seven (7) mountains and seven (7) rivers each.

Except the people in Jumbo Island, the ages of the persons of other islands are ten (10) thousand years. The age of the people of Jumbo Island is 125 years.

Specification of Measurement of The Sky According to Vedas and Puranas

Sky is spread over an area of 50 crore *Jojan.* The sun is one *lakh jojan* high from the Earth and the Moon is a one *lakh jojan* above the Sun. One *lakh jojan* above the Moon, there are Stars (*Taragun*). Above Taragun, there is Baikunth and on the door of the Baikunth, there are Dhoroop. All these are based on *(Aadhar Par) Namar Chakra.*

Dhoroop is thirteen (13) *lakh* jojan high from the Earth.

Bameergan Mountain is one *lakh jojan* high and on it is the pole (*Dhuri*) of the chariot of Suraj Narayan and on the other side of the pole, there is a rope tied to the Dhoroop star.

Badmanas Uttargar Mountains is in Pushkar Island, below it Earth is inhabited. There is a boundary wall *(Chardiwari)* on this mountain. The names of the four walls of the boundary wall are:

1. Rakin, 2. Dhajraj, 3. Baran, 4. Kabeer.

(Family tree of Brahmaji and the creation of Universe).

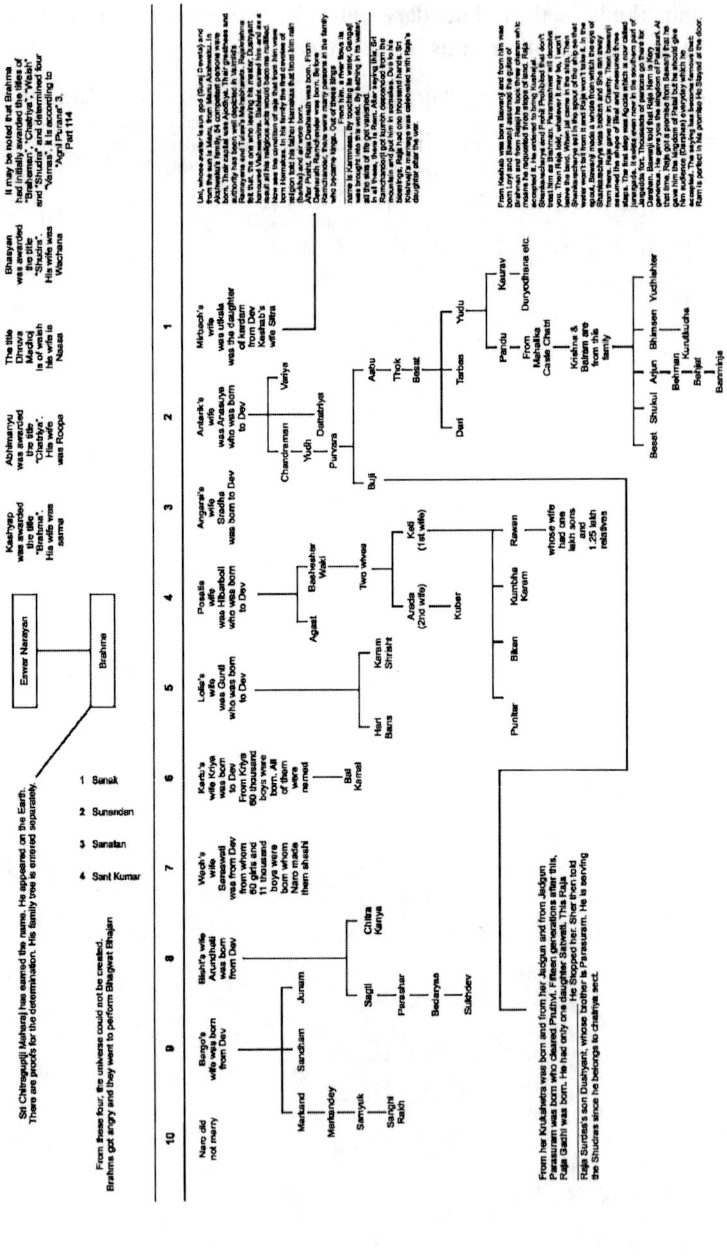

Chapter – II

Birth of Sri Chitraguptji with Progeny, Determination of Sect (*Varan*) and Precedents of the Court and Proofs of the Past Pandits of Kashmir, Pune, Nadiad etc.

The description of Sri Chitraguptji is in *Padam Purana's Uttar Khand* (Chapter) in three *adhyays* (Chapters). From it, a brief description is entered below:

Once in Prasaran, Song etc. and 88 thousand grandchildren of Brahmaji asked a question from *Sotji* that in which family Chitraguptji was born, give full description. *Sotji* got delighted and said that "Bhishm Pitamah (paternal grandfather) had put the same question to Agastji. I will describe it, listen".

One day, Bhishm Pitamah wished or saluted (*Namaskaar*) to Agastji and said "Maharaj, I have heard the description of four sects (*Varnas*) and four hermitage *(Ashram)* at many places in detail. Now, it is my wish to listen to the story of Sri Chitraguptji from your tender mouth that how was Sri Chitraguptji born and what is his religion *(Dharma)* and why is the name of his grandchildren "Kayasth" and how did the persons become very great intellectuals *(Maha Budhiman)* from each sect, (*Varan*). How did they become so influential? They used to be in the Royal Courts of all the Kings. They were well versed with the grammar of the *Shastras*. How did they become the nourishers of Brahmins? Who produced them? How many children did they produce? What is conduct and behaviour of that sect? Agastji told Bhishm Pitamah that he would describe the reason for the birth of Kayasths, the description of their grandsons and their religion. Be silent and listen. From the lotus of *Sri Parameshwar*, Brahmaji was created and Brahmaji created *Charachar*. From mouth, he created Brahmin, from *Bhuja* Kshatriya, from *Urud, vesh* and from feet, Shudra (Dalit) and assigned the authority of tasks related to each one of them. He called Ujjha Prajapat and told him "O son! I have put the burden of this Universe on your head. You enhance this progeny (*Shrishti*). Brahmaji after listening to the conversation of God (*Bhagwan*), gave a serious thought that he had created 14 generations. He also thought what would be their religion (*Dharma*) or non-religion (*Adharma*)? For this, eleven (11) thousand years were spent. Suddenly, from the body of Brahmaji, a boy with black eyes appeared and stood in front of Brahmaji with a pen and an inkpot in his hands. At that time, the attention (*Dhyan*) of Brahmaji got disturbed (*Choot gaya*). He looked at all the four sides, above and below. He saw a very handsome boy standing in front of him. He asked that boy "Who are you?" After hearing this, the boy told, "Maharaj, I was created from your body. Tell me my name. Show me my task. Determine my caste (*Varan*) and my livelihood. After listening to this, Brahmaji got very much delighted and said, O' my son, you have been created from my body *(aanth karan)* for nourishing the people, for imparting justice *(Dharma)* and for offering worship to the sons of Gods, to take care of Brahmins, to serve the destitute, to ponder over *Dharma* (justice) and *Adharma* (injustice). But before it, listen to my word (*Vachan*). Go to Avantipuri and offer worship (*Tapasya*) to Mahadev Mahakaal. After it, your name, your sect (*Varan*) your duty and the source of your livelihood would be told to you. After listening to such a word (*Vachan*) of Brahmaji, that boy, that is Chitraguptji went to Avantipuri (*Ujjain*) and worshipped Mahakaal Mahadev. Then, Brahmaji reached Avantipuri with eighty thousand chariots and performed the sacred thread ceremony (*Janeev*) of Chitraguptji and told that Brahmins etc. were created out of separate parts of his body and he also said that he (Chitraguptji) was created from his entire body. Due to this reason, he was named as Chitragupt and the name of his caste is "Kayasth", his sect (Varan) is Kshatri and Baglamukhi. Gayatri would be the incantation (*Mantra*).

Mantra and Chant Sri Debi Baglamukhi

त्र्पथबगलामुखी ॥
ॐह्रीं बगलामुखि सर्वदुठानां ॥ वाचंमुखं
मदं स्तंभय ॥ जिह्बां कीलय बुद्रिं विनाराय
ह्रीं ॐस्वाहा ॥
॥ इति जपन्पत्रः ॥
त्र्पस्य नारद्र ऋषिः बृहतीछंदः बगलामुखि
देवता बगलामुखी प्रीतये जपेविनियोगः ॥
॥श्रंगंन्यासः॥
इपंच पंच नवपंच दशभिर्मत्रार्णैं : बडंगं ॥
॥ अथध्यानं ॥
सौवर्णासन संस्थितांत्रिनयनां ॥ पीतांशु
कोल्लासिनीं ॥ हेमाश्रांगरुचिंशशांक मुकुटां
सच्चापकरत्रग्रयुतां हस्तैर्शुद्रर पाशवज्र -
रसनां संविश्रतीं श्रूषगां॥ व्याप्रागींबगला
मुरवीं त्रिजगतां संस्तंश्रनींचिंतयेतू ॥१॥
॥ लक्षनपः ॥
रष्पे र्हेमः ॥ पीतवासाः ॥पीतपुषानु
:॥पीत्तपुष्पैः पूजयेतू॥ हरिद्रामगिा
॥ इतिबगलामुखीः ॥

The people of your sect will be those who would chant Gayathri Mantra and the Gayathri Mantra of your sect is this according to Mahadev and Vedas.

न मोम गव तेवासदेवा पगीर्वांदा प धीन हीत न्ना विध्यू प्र चेद पातू

Your sect will perform sixteen duties as per the details entered in the third chapter of this book. You will occupy the seat of Dharam Raj and would determine about all the creation or birth and also decide *Dharma* (Justice) and *Adharma* (Injustice). In the same Puri, you will place one hundred pious heads of Brahmaji and worship. He was blessed with a daughter. He got angry and gave her to Suraj Narayan and started performing rites (*Prateesha*) for a son. At that time, he heard a sound from the Sky *(Aakashwani)* that he should sing devotional song (*Bhajan*) of *Sri Parmeshwar* with full concentration and his daughter would be married to a person whose family would never perish (*Nash*). His name would remain more than his son's name. Then Rakhji became peaceful and started reciting Bhagwat Bhajans with full concentration.

On one occasion, Sri Mahadevji and Parvati went to Suraj Narayan and asked "Whose daughter is she?" Suraj Narayan replied that she is the daughter of Sussar Markh and her name is Soubhavati. After hearing it, Mahadevji took Suraj Narayan with the girl and arrived in Avantipuri. He performed the marriage of Chitragupt with *Youdh Yudhiyan*. Later, Suraj Narayan performed the marriage of his eldest son, Sardaman's daughter, Nandini for the second time with Chitraguptji Maharaj.

Sri Brahmaji, Mahadevji, Parvati gave eighty eight thousand Rakh and proceeded to *Parlok* after blessing Chitraguptji. All the Gods started living in their own places and Chitraguptji stayed in Avantipuri. After a few days, Chitraguptji was blessed with four sons from the eldest son of Suraj Narayan's, Sardaman's daughter, Nandini, their names are: (1) Jogendhar, meaning Mathur, (2) Bhanu Prakash meaning Bhatnagar, (3) Ram Dayal meaning Sukhsen, (4) Dhruvadhoj meaning Srivastav.

From the daughter of Susar Markh, a daughter, whose name was Soubhavati, eight sons were born. They are: (1) Shyam Sundar meaning beautiful as the Sun, (2) Sarangdhar meaning Ast, (3) Dharam Dutt meaning Goud, (4) Sushist meaning Nigam, (5) Damodhar meaning Karan, (6) Deen Dayal meaning Ashthana, (7) Sadanand meaning Kulshrisht, (happy for all the time), and (8) Raghuram meaning Balmik. Later, Brahaspatji performed the sacred thread (*Janeev*) ceremony of all the eight sons. Sri Brahmaji performed the marriage ceremonies of all the twelve sons with Naag girls (*Kanyas*).

After this, Sri Brahmaji sent (1) Jogender (2) Bhanu Prakash (3) Ram Dayal and (4) Dharbadoj with Shyam Sunder with his two sons each in four directions and advised them to worship (1) Durga, (2) Jayanthi, (3) Shakambari and (4) Laxmiji. On getting instructions from Brahmaji, Jogender sent Shyam Sunder, Sarang Dhar to Brahmavrat which is spread from Kapila to Prayag in the East and from Jamuna to Ghagra in the West and in the North and in the South. Due to his stay there, Jogender's name became Mathur and Shyam Sunder's name was changed to Suraj Dhoj due to his stay in Magadh Des. For this reason, the Kings of Magadh Des are called Suraj Dhoj, Chera Sindh etc. and Sarang Dhar due to his stay in Brahmavrat, was called "Asht", Bhanup Prakash, due to his stay in Bhat Nagar meaning the city of Sehra Bahoon became Dharam Dutt and Susat. He stayed in Bhatnagar and sent Dharam Dutt to Gordes meaning Odisa, Bengala and sent Susat across Sarju. Due to staying here, the name of Bhanup Prakash became Bhatnagar and Dharam Dutt's name Goud. Susat's name became Nigam. Ram Dayal with Damodar and Deen Dayal went to Kabul and Khandahar. He stayed in Kabul and sent Damodhar to Karnataka Des on his behalf. He sent Deen Dayal to Nepal. Due to his stay in Nepal, Deen Dayal's name was changed into Eethan meaning native of Nepal. Ram Dayal's name became Shaksen meaning the Muslims who maintained army of Kabul. The one who lived in Karnataka that is Damodhar became Karan and Deen Dayal's name was changed as Eethan. Dharamdoj with Sadanand and Raghuram came to Srinagar where they fell in love with the daughter of Raja Naro Jeku Sibal Nada. He stayed in Srinagar and sent Sadanand on his behalf to Kalapikgram which is adjacent to Ambikapuri.

Due to Raghuram's stay in Chitrakot, from Sheesht Shudra Rameshwar, his name got changed as Balmik on account of it, this province is called Balmik Des.

Dharamodhoj was blessed with two sons with his first wife Narmada: (1) Devdat and (2) Ghanshyam. Dharmadhoj performed second marriage with Mansat, daughter of Samundar. He got two sons from her: (1) Dhanavantar and (2) Sarbagya. Both these sons acquired *Sukul* knowledge from Mahadevji. Mahadevji called Dharmadhoj along with his sons at the sea shore. Eighty thousand Rakh came there with

Brahmaji. Chitragupt, Yamraj also came there. Shakaracharja and Braspat performed the Vij *samskar* meaning *Jaganu Puneet* of both these sons. Then Samundar made Sarbagya, as the son of Dharam. Chitragupt became happy. After seeing the pleasure of the meeting, all the Gods went to their places and the daughter of Bidanon, whose name is Ajni, Samundar performed her marriage with Sarbagya. Dhanavantar married Raja Bran Nand's daughter, Amravati, from her, a son by name Sukeen with lotus eyes was born. Dhanavantar went to Pusatji and informed him about the birth of the son. He felt very happy and said "O Dhanavantar! Your son will do a lot of Ramji's work. He would be a great intellectual. Give him to me. I will keep him with me. He will be the minister of Rawan". After hearing this, Dhanavantar happily handed over Sukeen to Pusatji.

The differentiation among the genuine Kayasths and others is due to the sons of Dharamdoj. It means that those who belong to Devadutt and Ghanshyam are the real or genuine Kayasths and those who belong to the family of Dhanavantar and Sarbagya are others. It would be depicted from the following family tree:

FAMILY TREE

SRI BRAHMAJI JI

SRI CHITRAGUPT JI

1	2	3	4	5	6	7	8	9	10	11	12
Jogindar's name was changed as Mathur due to his stay in Magadh	The name of Bhanup Prakash became Bhatnagar due to his stay in Bhat Nagar	Ram Dayal's name was changed as Shaksen due to his stay in Kabul, Khandahar	Dharamduj's name was changed as Srivastav because of his stay in Sringar.	Shyam Sunder stayed in Magadh Des, so his name was Suraj Dhoj.	Sarang Dhar's name was changed as Ast because he stayed in Brahmaji-Varat	Dharam Dutt's name was changed as Goud due to their stay in Gordes (Odisha).	Sursat to outside border. Hence he was called Nigam.	Damodhar went to Karnatak, hence his name became Karan.	Deen Dayal went to Nepal and hence his name was changed as Eethan	Sadanand went to Kalapikgram and his name became Kulsrishit	Raghuram became Balmik due to his stay in Balmik Des.

Second Wife → **Dhanavantar *** → **Sukeen** →

Sarbagya*

First Wife → **Ghanshyam*** and **Devadutt***

He became the Minister (Diwan) of Rawan. When Lachmanji was called from Srilanka by Ramji, he desired and got Ramji's blessings. Ramji blessed him and told that his progeny will always continue with esteem and dignity.

* **Sarbagya and Dhanavantar** -- The family members of Dhanvantar and Sarbagya were called other Srivastav.

* **Ghanshyam & Devdutt** - The progency of both these persons became genuine or pure Srivastav.

The following table shows the names of the progeny of Sri Chitraguptji and the country for staying there, the other names became famous. It also shows the names of wives of Asat Dev.

FAMILY TREE

Serial Number.	Name of the son which existed before	Name of the place where the name changed due to the stay there	The second name which is now famous	Names of the girls who got married	Name of the Ast Dev who is to be worshipped	Number of sons born	
1.	2	3	4	5	6	7	8
1.	Jugender	Mathura	Mathur	Padmini	Durga Ji	1	It may be noted that Dharamdhoj married twice, the name of one wife was Narmada and the other was Mansat. From Narmada were born Srivastav which were genuine and those born to Second wife were other Srivastav
2.	Bhanup Prakash	Bhat Nagar	Bhatnagar	Malithi	Jayanthi	2	
3.	Ram Dayal	Kabul, Khandahar	Shaksen	Rambha	Shakambari	3	
4.	Dhraramdhoj	Srinagar	Srivastav	Narmada and Mansat	Laxmiji	4	
5.	Shyam Sunder	Magadh Des	Suraj Dhoj	Bhoukamini	Durgaji	1	
6.	Sarang Dhar	Brahmajivarat	AST	Bhujanghi	Durgaji	1	
7.	Dharam Dutt	Gordes	Goud	Pankaj Akji	Jayanthi	2	
8.	Susat	Beyond Sarju	Nigam	Gandaki	Jayanthi	2	
9.	Damodhar	Karnatak	Karan	Kanklas Sona	Shakambari	3	
10.	Deen Dayal	Asthan	Eehan	Asgandhani	Shakambari	3	
11.	Sadanand	Kalapikgram	Kul Srisht	Kamkala	Laxmiji	4	
12.	Raghu Ram	Balmik Des	Balmik	Saju Bagany	Laxmiji	4	

It may be mentioned that in the book "Brahmaji Darshan" at serial number 2, dated 25th November 1824 and at serial number 57 dated 14th May 1876, determination of the Kayasths has been made. This sect has been determined as Kshatriya by the Pandits of Kasi, Kashmir, Jumbo, Prayag, Lucknow, Agra and Pune. A similar determination has been made in Kayasth Samachar, printed at Lucknow, publication number 6, month of November 1878. Accordingly, the decision of Raja Lachman Singh, Deputy Collector Bahadur, Bulund Shehar got cancelled in which he had declared Kayasths as Shudras.

In the case of Govt. of India versus the previous Pandits, the above mentioned High Court etc. and as per the other precedents of the Shastra, of 8th February 1877, the Deputy Collector on seeing the book "Kayasth Ethnology" written by Munshi Kalay Pershad, Advocate, in the court of Judicial Commissioner of Awadh published an advertisement on 15th May 1877 that due to ignorance, he had written Kayasth community as Shudras but now it has become completely certain that the Kayasths belonging to Chitragupt family and Chandrasen family are not Shudras but they are Kshatriya Doj sect (Varan). From the book "Kalpavaram and Kayasth Banshiya" written by Pradeep M. Sungta, it is confirmed that 'Kayasths' are from Kshatri sect and this sect of Kayasths has been in vogue for the past so many years. The progenitor of this family is Sri Chitragupt Maharaj, whom all the three sects (Varanas) salute and offer sacrifice *(Aahoti).*

(Chitra-e-Chitragupt Aatma)

Dattatriji told that all their details to Bishopji in *Dabdam Purana* and in Acharya Nay Tantra also the description of the progeny of Chitragupt is entered. Mahadevji who is of 64 Tantra, is also mentioned. In Bhoom Singha also, it is written that Kayasths came into being from the body (*Kaya*) of Sri Brahmaji. In Aayeen-e-Akbari (biography of Emperor Akbar the Great), the royal duties of Kayasth sect are entered. In *'Seeru Tantra'*, it is entered that Maharaj Chitragupt revealed in Veda's Upanishad. Maharaj Chitragupt made Inder Jal. Tantrakak Srivastav Sribans said that Amar Singh Maharaj compiled Amarkosh (Dictionary) and helped (*Teka*) in compiling grammar (*Vyakaran*). Maharaj Saran Kamal compiled Arithmetic (*Ganit Vidya*), Numerology

(*Ank Vidya*) and accounting or the knowledge of sales and purchase accounts (*Baich Ganit Vidya*).

In olden days, in this manner, many great persons (*Mahatma*) were knowledgeable individuals meaning scholars or intellectuals or wisemen or educated. At many places, there are temples and idols of Sri Chitragupt Maharaj. Brahmins worship in these temples and take his *'Prasad'* (food offered before an idol or God). Kayasths essentially worship *Katik Sadi Dosaj*. According to 'Dhaniyajan Sangna', in such an act, pen and inkpot are also worshipped. It is also entered in *Guru Puran's Adhyay* (Chapter) that Maharaj Chitragupt is Kayasth. He sees sinners and the righteous persons (*Dharmatmas*). It is mentioned at page number 22 of *'Aakal Rutuvu'*.

In Aachar Nibratay Tantra, it is also written that Raja Suvig asked Sri Sat Parsi who would be the companion of the Brahmins in '*Kalyug*'? He told 'Kayasth'. To say that all these talks or matters of Raja Suvig and Sat Parsi of Brahm Muhurat Purana, Section-50 is also mentioned.

Hence, from all these conversations or descriptions, it is proved that Chitraguptji's family belongs to Kshatri sect (Varana). If they are termed as 'Shudras', then, where will be the Brahminism of the Brahmins, won't they turn 'Shudras'? It is entered in Avadh Newspaper, serial number 255 dated 27th October, 1879 that the Judge of Patna in the case number 26 of 1879 dated 9th October, 1879 pronounced the judgment mentioned, which contained the arguments about the sect (Varan) of 'Kayasths' that the procedure for adoption of children (*Mutabanna*) in Srivastav Kayasths was entered which is according to *Doj Bartiyon* in which there is no need to perform any rites and rituals as Shudras (Now referred or called as ST/SC/Backward Classes) do.

In this court case, the major evidence is about the fact that Chitraguptji belongs to Kshatriya family. Rani Kunwar *Madesa's* father had the sacred thread (*Janeev*). He used to perform rites and rituals (*Hom*) according to the *'mantar'* of Vedas. Many Kayasths perform '*Hom*' in the same manner. This is absolutely prohibited for the Shudras. It is possible that the Kayasths of the present time may be hereditary Kshatris which means such Kshatriyas who perform all the rites and rituals which are essential for Kshatris. There is no doubt about it that Kayasths are till now Kshatris. They have not accepted the rites and rituals of the Kshatris so far. After seeing the expressions of the famous Pandits of Banaras about their following of Vedas, Dharam Shastra etc., we got full confidence that the father of complainant or plaintiff belonged to Kshatri sect (*Varan*) and not Shudra.

The statements of the Pandits which the defendants or respondents of the court case got recorded wanted treacherously to give wrong meaning or interpretations to the *Aslokas*. Most of the references they quoted were such that they were not amenable to reason in the matters pertaining to business and transactions. The progeny of *Bansiya* and *Bedhiya* alone are called Kayasths. Since all of them are not from the Chitraguptji's family *(Bansiya)*. Only on the basis of similarity of names of the plaintiff or complainants or defendants, it cannot be called Chitraguptji's Bansiya Kayasths are also Shudras.

All those Chandrasen Banshi Kayasths who are born from Kshatri father and mother also can't be called "Shudras". Whatever respect and value the Kayasths get proves that the Kayasths can't be Shudras.

Chotu Ram has admitted that the compiler of "Amarkosh", Amar Singh was a famous author but whatever he wrote about the sect (Varana) of the Kayasths does not mean that the Chitragosh Kayasths should also be classified in the same category as Kayasths.

As per the above mentioned reasons, our plea is that the complainant's father and the respondent are not the Shudras but they were from the Duj Baran Kayasth sect (Varana). At the same time, it also gets explicit that many Rajputs, about whom there is no doubt that they are Kshatris. They do not wear the sacred thread *(Janeev)*. Many of them do not perform the same rites and religious duties, but, due to these reasons, it can't be said that they are not Kshatris. Many of their relatives wear *Janeev* and perform religious rites. On account of these reasons, our opinion is that whatever law is applicable for the progeny of Chitraguptji would be applicable to the complainant and the respondent and not the law of the Shudras. The names of Kings who ruled as Kshatris are as follows:

In Kayasth Bans Pardeep and Aachar *Tarni Tantra*, it is written that in Rang Des, the rule of Kayasth family has been in vogue for a long period.

In *"Aachar Nirnay Tantra",* it is written that two thousand years after 'Kalyug' a famous king belonging to Kshatri family (Varana) by name Sreemansujag had established his capital at a place called 'Bural'. A document *(Tamar Patra)* written during that period was found by the British during excavation. The rule of this dynasty continued till 811 A.D. After this, Maharaj Udit Soor who is also called Urdsri ruled the country. He was a great Kayasth Kshatri emperor. In the book of Gola George, he has been written as the ruler of the world.

In the 9th section (sutra) of *"Theerath Adhyan",* of vedant, it is written that Udit Soor was a very fortunate or prosperous king, under him was this beautiful and picturesque Universe Chitrangini Sansar.

In the Chapter of *Senapati* (Army Commander), it is written that there were 123330 *Sawars,* 1158, *Cavalry men,* 170, Bodha meaning wrestler *(Pahelwan)* and elephant riders were 4460. Those who set fire were 1,04,400 soldiers. After him, a king by name Pal who was a Kayasth Kshatri ruled the country. The area which was under the jurisdiction of the British pertaining to Gordes (presently Odisha) was named as Bengala.

Raja Sanjay Sen who is also known as Sukh Sain was the Ast Kayasth King.

In the history of British Bengal compiled by Mormam Sahab, it is written that in 1430, the king of Bengal was from the family of Raja Sen. His headquarters was in Getur City. He belonged to Kayasth Goud community. His headquarters was Nadia Shantipur in Trihat District. His age was 80 years. After him, king Qutubuddin came from Delhi. All these facts prove that the association of Chitraguptji's family of Kayasths with Kshatris sect (Varan) and their participation in governance and Vedic duties. There is a mention of Chitraguptji in *Bhavishya Purana.* In *Vigyan Tantra* also, Brahmaji has called Kayasths from Kshatri Varana. There is a description in *Naasket Purana* also and in *Tantra Mahodaya*, there is a description of Chitraguptaji's Gayatyri and in "*Zaat Back Nirnay Aur Shudra Kamalakar*" there is a mention of Kayasths.

In Aranyaka *Mahatam Askand Purana*, also there is a description of Kayasths.

The second judgment of the court is also entered as precedent in which it has been proved that Kayasths belong to the family of Chitraguptji and their sect is Kshatri.

The English translation of the extract of the judgment pronounced by Banshidhar Sahab, Magistrate was produced by the Complainant in the Court to prove that Kayasths are from Duj in which previous details of Puranas, Dharma Shastras with Sathakshara were entered.

Among all, the following translation is of *Padam Purana Srishti Khand.* In order to find out good and bad acts of a man, at the time of his birth, Brahmaji pondered over it for a moment.

A person like him was born. He was named as Chitragupt.

He was appointed to work with Dharmaraj to write good and bad deeds of human beings. From among the wise Gods he excelled in esteem. He was the one who always used to get food in this world. Due to this reason, people always offer him food (*Aahooti*). Since he was created out of the powers of Brahmaji, his caste was therefore, called Kayasth. Most of the Kayasths of his family (*Gotra*) are in fact on the Earth.

From this extract (selection) it becomes evident that the status of the Kayasth as the progeny of Chitraguptji. In *Bhavishya Purana*, there is a saying, in which Brahmaji himself addresses Chitraguptji and tells the following:

"You were born out of our (my) body. You were, therefore, named as Kayasths and known as Chitragupt on the Earth. In order to discriminate between good and bad, be with Dharam Raj, with my permission you be my son and Kshatri sect (Varana) which is appropriate for justice, follow it. By paying attention/concentration on the Earth, increase your family". However, according to Kayasth ethnology, the description of the Kayasths is as entered in *Puranik Shastra*. Whatever difference is there about the orthodoxy of the Puranas, it seems appropriate that from the ancient time, if Kayasths are not equal to Chitralok, they have been treated in the nearest time in performing the religious duties. It is said that this situation continued till the foreigners conquered this country. Muslim conquerors of India provided ease and opportunities to many people of every rank, the Kayasths are no exception. The rules were very strict. They continued to follow these rules for the past periods. They came in contact with a community, whose religious rituals were completely different from them. As a consequence of this amalgamation, many persons found it easy to break their traditions and rituals. In this manner, whatever changes took place in the community, they were well known to them. Due to these reasons, contacts developed between these two communities. As a result of these contacts, hybrid children were born but right from the beginning, they continued their associations with the Hindus.

In the original Kayasths, like the other Duj Sects, marriages take place within the same community or the persons of equal status. All the rituals are performed as per Shastra. Second marriage of the widow is prohibited. The funeral rites are performed only by the progeny of the deceased persons or the members of the right descent.

Those who are born due to the matrimonial alliances with other communities are treated as excluded from the Kayasth community. Although some of such rich persons of Kayasth community are under the pressure from such persons but they are worried about their origin. Such persons do not eat the food cooked by the genuine Kayasths. They don't even think of touching this food. Such traditions are not found among the Shudras. Devoid of such attitude is the symbol of the Shudras. As far as the attitude is concerned, it has not been argued by the complainants that the Kayasths of the present period are Shudras since they don't wear the sacred thread (Janeev). They do not recite the incantation of *Gayatri*. First of all, this argument holds good for a few persons of Kayasth community. There is no denying of this comment but there are a few exceptions also.

Secondly, no reference of any rule of Shastra has been provided under which the status of a Duj gets degraded and he is associated with the Shudras not only virtually but actually quoting thousands of such bases or reasons, they are counted as Dujas. They do not wear sacred thread. In *Dharam Shastra*, three kinds of duties are enumerated. They are as follows:

First good or virtuous character *(Aachaar);* second behaviour *(Vyohaar);* third repentance *(Prayeshchit)*.

If any person (Duj) is not able to comply with these injunctions *(Ahkaam),* he has to take advantage of the rules mentioned for compensation. If he has such kind of wishes, he would be called a Shudra with contempt. If he performs religious duties perfectly, he could be viewed righteously. However, the rules of inheritance *(Virasat)* and other matters pertaining to Civil Court would remain the same which were assigned to Duj in the beginning as per the Kayasth ethnology and *Shastra.*

In section number 335 of the book of conduct, it is entered that the Kayasths are clerks (*Munshis*) and *Mutasaddi* (Accountant or Secretary). Kings like them very much. Narad Barasti and Biyasji's quotation is entered in *Satakshara Udveer Matrodi*, that the Accountant is one of the members of the King's Court. He sits to impart justice. Accountant *(Mahasib)* used to be counted as *Sharat*, which meant that he used to be well versed in *Meamam* and Grammar *(Vyakaran)* etc. and he used to understand Vedas. According to Takshra Valvaha, *Aslok* number 2 accountant used to be originally from Duj community. In those days, almost all the Pandits right from Kashmir to Kanyakumari hold the same opinion. The complainant did not prove against it.

I, therefore, deem it proper that as per *Dharam Shastra*, Kayasths should be determined in Duj community. Due to this reason, the bastard or illegitimate son is not entitled to inherit from his assumed father *(Farzi Baap).* From this, it should not be construed that Kayasths are absolutely *(Sareeh)* or genuinely Kshatris. In fact, they themselves do not claim that they are included in warrior community. For the purpose of this case, only it is required that they are *Duj* (Bigamist or a man who marries a second woman) and in this context, the foundation/ basis of their claim seems to be appropriate / correct / genuine. In the context of sect (*Varan*), it is a matter worth considering that there are four specific sects, which means, Brahmin, Kshatri, Vesh and Shudra about whom it is mentioned that they were created from the mouth, arms, thighs and feet of Brahmaji and according to the quotation mentioned above, the Kayasths were created out of the body *(Kaya)* of Brahmaji meaning from the entire body.

Thus, primarily, the Kayasths could not have been included in any of the four sects and in this court case; it has not been proved that a specific sect (*Varana*) has been determined for them (*Kayasths*). On the other hand, it seems that due to their creation from the entire body of Brahmaji, there exist all the rights and privileges in them. Since only four sects (*Varanas*) have been determined, there is no mention of the fifth sect. The duties Brahmaji has assigned to them are those of the Kshatris. They, therefore, could be presumed as Kshatris, which means they are the second category of Kshatris according to their sect.

The descriptions of the earlier Pandits which is mentioned in the Kayasth ethnology, as Kayasths.

Earlier Pandits who have written (entered) in the Kayasth ethnology and appeared in the courts. They were attested or certified under oath by great Pandits and Mahatmas as right. Their expressions or statements were included in the files of the documents and their copies.

In Kayasth ethnology at page 51 in the translation and gist of the earlier number 60 written by Pandit Sundar Deva in the court of Agra dated 15th July, 1861 it was mentioned that Kayasths are not Shudras. They are of Kshatri sect (Varana). Bastard son does not inherit property.

According to *Satakshara Udveer Matrodi*, otherwise under the pretext of getting property, he keeps widow with him like Shudras do.

Pandit Nityanand who was sent by Babu Raghunath Pershad Mahajan of Benaras presented the original *pothi shastra* '*Kamdhenu'* and got its extract included in the file of the Civil Court of Mirzapur. By presenting the extract of Shastra, which was included in the file after getting it certified got the opinion, that the Kayasths are from the family of Chitraguptji and they are not Shudras.

Pandit Tasi Ram Duji, Professor of Sanskrit Grammar of Govt. College, Banaras is an old Saro Brahmin. He is recognised as the chief of the Pandits of Panch Goud in Banaras. He saw the original books and certified / attested the extract / selection included in the file and mentioned that the Kayasths of Chitraguptji and Chandrasen families as the Kshatri caste (*Varana*) and gave testimony/witness that he has seen thousands of Kayasths wearing the sacred thread (*Janeev*). At page-59, Pandit Dhonda Raj Shastri, and Pandit Bal Shastri, Professor of Dharam Shastra of Govt. College, Banaras attested the statement of the earlier pandits of Banaras that Raja Ram Shastri Manu, former teacher of Dharam Shastra of Govt. College Banaras also put his signature on it and offered testimony that the extract included in the file is according to the original Sanskrit books and mentioned that the Kayasths belonging to Chitraguptji and Chandrasen families are from the Kshatri caste (Varana). At page 62, the statement of the earlier Pandits, is that the progenitor (Morisan) of Chitraguptji and Chandrasen families were Kshatri Varan Duj (the sects of bigamists or the persons who married two wives) and the duties assigned to them are similar to the duties assigned to Kshatris.

Earlier statements of Pandits of Pune dated 1851 Bakrami equivalent to 1771 A.D. in which there is a reference of *Askand Purana*, Shudar Kamlakar, and Kayasth Pradeep written by Gaga Bhut etc. and on it there are 49 signatures of the pandits.

At page 64 of the statement of the previous pandits of Kasi dated 1844 in which there is a reference of *Padam Purana*, *Srisht Khand, Askand Purana*, Ritika Mahayam, and *Bhavishya Purana* etc. and in *Shlok* of *Bhavishya Purana*, there is a mention that Kayasths are from the Kshatri caste (Varan) and on it there are signatures of 8 Pandits.

There is a statement of the earlier Pandits of Bengal recorded in 1844 A.D. in which there is a reference of *Padam Purana, Askand Purana*, and Shudra Kamlakar etc. There are signatures of 49 Pandits on it. It was included previously in the Court of Gorakhpur and these have been published in Bangla script (language) in the book named 'Kayasth Katu' printed in 1844, also in the book 'Kayasth Sangatha' printed in 1875.

At page 70, there is a statement of the earlier pandits of Mathuraji on which there are signatures of Ananth Acharaj Chaturvedi, Busharmana Amar Lal Joshi and 22 other Pandits. Page 72 contains the statements of the Jumbo Pandits who are like the river of the capital of the state, there is Raghunathji Temple. On each *Ekadashi,* meeting (Sabha) of pandits is held. In this meeting, the document (*Patra*) of the Pandits which contained the songs (*Bhajans*) of *Askand Purana, Padam Purana, Pataal Khand* etc. were approved and 43 pandits signed on it.

At page 73, it is mentioned that Maharaja Dharam Raj Sri Ranbeer Singh Bahadur organised a meeting or function (*Sabha*) of all the

Pandits especially in Kashmir on the day of *Ekadashi* and discussed the caste (*Varana*) of Kayasths and all the Pandits who had the knowledge of *Vedas* and *Shastras* and they were the scholars of Smurti Dharam Shastra and puranas after seeing the signatures of 96 pandits of Kashiji and Jumbo and their behaviour *(Vyasthav)* agreed and said that in Puranas, the families of Chitraguptji and Chandrasen have been recognised as Kshatris and 332 pandits signed on it.

Sri Chitragupt Maharaj is recognised as the progenitor of the Kayasths in the *Padam Purana, Srishti Khand, Bhavishya Purana, Askand Purana, Ahilya Kamadhenu, Tantra Mahodaya, Aachar Nirnay, Tantra Gasal, Tantra Guru Puran and Bhoom Sangya* etc. are recognised as Kshatri caste of the Kayasths. The caste of their progeny would also be recognised as Kayasths. It is not that the ancestor belonged to one caste and his son belonged to another caste/sect (*Varana*).

Chapter – III

Description of the Rites Pertaining to the Caste, which have been Written Briefly in the Vedas

Saints *(Rishis)* have written the rites differently according to their opinions and these rites are similar and equal for the entire caste. The method of worshipping Sri Chitraguptji Maharaj and the descriptions of the sub-division of caste *(Gotra)* of 12 members of progeny of Sri Chitraguptji Maharaj according to *Bhavishya Puranas* are written in the 12th section of Uttarakhand.

The First rite : When the woman attains puberty, from the fifth day of menstruation to the sixteenth day of menstruation, the rite to be offered is the *manateri* prayer which is called '*Bishivadhara*' and the sacred verses (*Mantras*) of the Gods should be chanted to offer worship to Gods. She should offer *Shradh* (ritual of offering food) of curd, ghee and honey in the form of ball and eat it and also offer alms (*Dakshina*) to Brahmins according to affordability. It is the generosity or the municificence (*Joad*) of the duty or obligation.

The Second rite: In the third month of pregnancy, she should be with Pon Soon Vastu. For three months, pregnancy will be in the gestation period, which means, it will be in the form of a lump of flesh like a bubble (*Hubaab*). The fourth month of pregnancy is the time when it assumes the shape of a human being. During this time, the manetari' worship. *Bishivadhara* and the sacred verses (*Mantras*) of the Gods should be chanted. During this time, *Sradh* (sacred food) and alms should be offered to Brahmins. After performing all these acts or rituals, take a lash (*Kasha*) and a branch of banyan tree which is called *Anguma,* dip it in water and make the woman drink it with the right hand in such a quantity that some of it should reach the stomach of the woman. For this worship or prayer (*Poojan*) there is permission of the first shastra, the second is that very often, a boy is born.

The Third rite is called *Santoneen* when the pregnancy is of six months, it is a tradition (*Dastur*) that hands and feet are formed. The man (Husband) should perform manetari rituals (manetari pooja) as mentioned above and fill the edge of the sari (*Pallu*) of the woman (wife) with flowers, sweets and ripe coconut.

The Fourth rite is called *Jaat Karma* (a ceremony performed on the birth of a child before cutting umbilical cord). After the birth of the boy or the girl, after cutting umbilical cord, man (Husband) after performing *manetari pooja* etc. should write something three times with a thin metallic bar or needle of gold dipped in honey on the tongue of the child.

The Fifth rite is called *"Nama Karan"* (the ceremony of naming the child after the birth or giving a name). When eleven days are passed after the birth of the child, *manetari* pooja should be performed taking the first letter of the planet in whose house/phase/stage, the child was born, the name should be selected after joining the next word after the first word of the star/planet. The following are the words, which should be joined after the first word of the star: da, ya, ba, ra, sa____ da.

हयवर त्उः यमड एानः जचघढधः जवगडद

The Sixth rite is called *"Nashkareen"* when the boy enters the fourth month, manetari pooja should be performed and he should be taken out of the house. He should be made to see (*Darshan*) the Sun (Suraj Narayan). An earthen pot or plate should be filled with milk and it should be kept for the Sun as offering.

The Seventh rite is called *"Anna Parosan"* when the boy starts sixth month, he should be fed with food made of food grains after performing manetari pooja.

The Eighth rite : In the third year, according to the tradition of the family, *manetari pooja* etc. should be performed and after that "*Mundan*" (the ceremony of shaving the child's head for the first time) should be done.

The Ninth rite is called *"Karan Beda"*. The ceremony of piercing the ear of the child for the first time. It should be performed during the third or the fifth year of child's age.

The Tenth rite is called *"Ubayan"* which means the thread ceremony or the ceremony to tie the sacred thread (*Janeev*). It should be performed when the eleventh or twelfth year of the child begins. It should be done after performing manetari pooja. At the time of performing thread (*Janeev*) ceremony, there is a tradition of Brahmins that they ask for alms. Kayasths should not do this.

The Eleventh rite : After eleven years of age, Moon sighting (*Deedar-e-Maah*) should be done.

The Twelfth rite : After twelfth year of age, he should observe fast (*Barat*) and start worship or religious observance.

The Thirteenth rite: From the age of twelfth year, one should remain *Brahmachari* (Ascetic) till he finishes the study of the Vedas.

The Fourteenth rite : After the eighteenth year, the stage is called "*Samavarthan*" which means that one should offer worship to the mentor/teacher or the spiritual guide and seek permission from the mentor to lead family life.

The Fifteenth rite : To marry.

The Sixteenth rite : *Anteyeshti,* meaning performing the funeral rites of a deceased person. But, from the same source (*Sutra*), it is learnt that if the earlier duties or religious rites have not been performed on time, they should be done before performing the thread (*Janeev*) ceremony since without performing the previous rites, thread ceremony can't be performed. Therefore, most of the Brahmins whether Gouds or *Dravids*, perform earlier rites at the time of performing the thread ceremony. In the same manner, in Kayasths also, the *purohit* (family priest) performs all the earlier religious rites before performing the thread ceremony (*Zunnardari*) since we (Kayasths) do not know Sanskrit, we do not know all these rites.

The method of worshipping Chitraguptji Maharaj and the time is described briefly in *Padam Puranas*, which is in the third part of Uttarakhand. Sotji says that after hearing Sotakji's saying Bhishma Pitamaha asked Agastji the birth of Maharaj Chitraguptji and other details, he heard from him. He says in what manner and how the worship should be offered to Sri Chitraguptji Maharaj and what kind of fruit (benefit) one gets for worshipping Chitraguptji. After listening to it, Agastji told that the fruit (benefit) of the story of Chitraguptji and his worship is in the story of Raja Sudas and listen to that story. Raja Sudas was a very famous King in the dynasty of Suraj Vanshi Kings. He was the great sinner. In his body (personality), absolutely there was no sense of *Dharma* or justice. So much so that in his kingdom, he had released a notification that nobody should give alms to the poor or perform *Hom* or worship (*Pooja*). After seeing this order, people went to places wherever they got refuge and the Brahmins who remained there, their prayers and worships were abandoned completely.

Once all the Brahmins consulted each other and came to persuade the king. The king did not accede to the persuasions of the Brahmins. The Brahmins then, cursed him that he may turn *demon or evil* spirit. After getting the curse from the Brahmins, the king turned into a demon and started wandering on the entire Earth. One day, he barged into the house of a Kayasth on the day of *Kartik's Shukul Paksh Jam Duwtiya.*

Kayasths had assembled there and they were worshipping Sri Chitraguptji Maharaj. Raja Sudas took all the *flowers* and offered them to the idol of Sri Chitraguptji. Chitraguptji felt very happy and all the sins of Raja Sudas vanished. He, therefore, came back to his kingdom and ruled there for ten thousand years. When he died, the devotees made him face Yamraj (the god who takes away lives of people). At that time, Chitraguptji Maharaj came to his rescue and saved him. Except offering flowers to the idol of Sri Chitraguptji Maharaj, he had no virtues to his credit in the world. Sri Chitraguptaji Maharaj told Dharma Raj that Raja Sudas had worshipped him on the occasion of Jam Duwitya. He has, therefore, to go to *'Bishnalok'*. With the permission of Dharma Raj, Sri Chitraguptji Maharaj arranged to send Raja Sudas in *Bishnalok* and said that he has to worship Sri Chitraguptji twice a year in *Bishnalok.* Once to the Moon on the occasion of *Kartik Shukla Paksh* and the second time, *Chait Shukla Paksh's Moon* (The second day of the Lunar fortnight). The method of worship is that a good square altar should be constructed and a *Kalas* (pinnacle/conicas or rounded top of a dome) of gold, silver, copper or clay filled with sugar *sherbet*, should be created. Garlands of flowers should be put on it. Its mouth (end of edge) should be tied with a silk cloth. This pinnacle should be similar to that which is erected for offering worship to Brahmaji and Ganeshji. A tree made of acacia (*Babool*) or any other wood should also be erected on the altar. On this tree, the idol of Sri Chitraguptaji Maharaj made of gold, silver, copper or red sanders should be installed after giving bath of red sanders to it. Worship/prayer should be offered with sandal, *varhat*, flowers according to the method and all types of *naved* should be kept. Rice, white sugar, *laddu* (a kind of sweetmeat in the shape of ball) and all kinds of sweets should be offered to the deity. At the time of offering *naved*, the idol should be covered with a silk cloth. The chanting of Chitraguptji should be done with utmost devotion.

While worshipping, one should take four rounds (circumambulation) of the idol. Kettledrum (*Danka*) should be beaten. *Shankh* (conch, large shell), *mirdang* (small drum) and various kinds of musical instruments should be played. Songs and dance programmes should be organised. *Prasad* (food offered to propitiate or please God) should be given to Brahmins. Eat the food with the members of the family after keeping it on the head.

In the Duj of Kartik's Shukla Paksh Jamunaji fed Maharaj in her house due to this reason, the portion (*Tathva*) is named as *"Jam Dwita"*.

One should eat in it with the hands of his sister and should give some alms. If a person does not have his own sister, then the ritual of *"Jam Dwita"* should be performed by the cousin (daughter of father's brother) or any woman with whom the relationship of sister could be established. He told Bhishma Pitamah that he himself should worship Chitraguptji. Through his favour you won't be worried of the horror of death and those who offer prayer to Chitraguptji in this manner, would get wealth, justice (*Dharma*) etc. and will have all sorts of comforts, in this world and release from rebirth. Ultimately, he would go to the world (*Lok*) of Narayana. Anyone who would organise programme for listening to the story of Chitraguptji and offer worship to him, he would be comfortable in this world so long as he is alive. At the end of his life, he would be in the best abode/paradise of Vishnu (*Paramdham*). He will also get an opportunity to bathe in the river Sri Gangaji in Prayag on moonlight (*Makara*) on the occasion of Solar eclipse in Kurukshetra, bathing in Kashiji on the occasion of Lunar eclipse and *Tuladaan* (alms equal to distributor's weight) etc. The benefit (*phal*) one gets out of *Tuladaan* programme, is on account of the worship offered to Chitraguptji, organising to listen to his story and by reading it.

Don't presume Bhishma Pitamah as grass, Govan (cow) as an animal, Gangaji as river, gold as metal and Kayasths as Shudras. These Kayasths have been created out of Sukul (belonging to noble ancestry of Brahmaji). Sotji says that after telling Sonik the method of worship of Chitraguptji and Mahatma Agast, Bhishma Pitamah immersed in *Antardhyan* (deep and profound meditation) and Bhishma Pitamah, according to the advice of Agastji, organised the feeding (*Bhojan*) of Sri Chitraguptji as per the above mentioned method. At that time, Sri Chitraguptji made an appearance and was delighted with Bhishma Pitamah and blessed him (*Aashirvad*) that Bhishma Pitamah, that he will not have the horror of death. After saying this, he went into deep meditation. These details are entered in *Padam Purana* and Uttarakhand 11th Chapter concerning the method of offering worship to Sri Chitraguptji Swami.

Description of the Sub-sects 12 progeny of Sri Chitraguptji Maharaj, which is, entered in Kalp (sacred) Sutra (quotations) Ved's 15th System (Sidhant)

Chart

Present Residential Status	***Sub-Sector (Gotra)***	***Parvar***	***Branch (Sakha)***
Mathur, Mathura and Hyderabad	Kaasib	Jamdugni Bharadwaj	Madhoni
Bhatnagar, outskirts of Delhi	Bhat	Angars-Gotham	Uttari

(*Contd...*)

Saxena, Lucknow and Bans Bareily	Hans	Bhargav Badsu	Sakali
Sribastab (Srivastav), Banaras, Bihar and Chapra	Sri Harsh	Godha Maliatha	Teetari
Suraj Dhuj, Buland Shehar	Sobhar	Angars Baraspat	Karsi
Asht, Gayaji, Patna	Bishisht	Indra Prabha Bhardoshu	Murasi
Goud, Banaras, Chiryakot, Azamgarh.	Goutham	Angars Abas goutham	Sokali
Nigam, Khandwa district Danmar	Mandab	Bhargav Chawan Aapnoo	Saktani
Karan, Sambalpur and Gayaji	Vallabh	Bachaspati, Bhardwaj	Surasi
Asthana, Agra, Lucknow Kamitabani	Sabhar	Braspat, Bhargav	
Kulshrisht, Agra	Barat	Mandhat Ambarish Nas	Padmathi
Balmik, Surat Barkhavati	Balmik	Surangi Samikya	
Nanabhai, Haridas	—	Bhargav Chaonoon	—
Judge, High Court, Mumbai	—	Aapnoon	—

Chapter - IV

Family Tree and Description of the Family of Compiler of this Book, his Relatives and other Members of the Community

Devotee Khoobchand, compiler of this book, resident of Banaras city, locality Prahalad Ghat, son of Lala Raghuveer Dayal Singh, son of Macharam Qanoongo of pargana Zamania, District Ghazipur, community Kayasth Srivastava otherwise known as Pandiya which is now called Dildaar Nagar, recently arrived in the city of Hyderabad Deccan, working as Munshi (clerk) at the territory of Thomas Palmer Sahab Bahadur Councillor, by writing the genealogy and the details of family and other esteemed brethren and relatives leaves this, as a memorial for others.

The progenitor of the compiler of this book had three sons; out of which the name of one son is not known. Our grandfather was Janab Lala Macharam Sahab. He married two wives. From the first marriage was Lala Shiv Dayal Singh Sahab and from the second marriage was Lala Raghuveer Dayal Singh, Lala Gur Dayal Singh and two daughters. The first daughter got married to Lala Ram Baksh Singh of Kangroha village, Chosha Pargana, Shahabad District. The second daughter got married to Lala Mohan Lal of Cheethapur village, Ghazipur District.

Earlier, our grandfather, Lala Macharam worked as *Qanoongo* (former functionary who collected revenue) at Zamania Pargana of

Ghazipur District. He was appointed by the kings of Lucknow. My grandfather had three brothers. Out of these three brothers, one brother got his share of property located at Akhandagarhi village mortgaged with the inheritors of Dildaar Khan who was a Khoja in the Court of the King of Lucknow. When our grandfather heard of it, he got this property released from the mortgage. After a few years as per usual habit, the same person sold out his share of property to the inheritors of Dildaar Khan again. At that time, the inheritors of Dildaar Khan attacked, for getting the right to get possession of the property in the said village. But, our grandfather along with other elders defended, fought with him and did not allow their entry into the village. The inheritors of Dildaar Khan sought help from Dildaar Khan Khoja and he started sending a large Royal army. It started reaching troop by troop as a reinforcement. The battle started from the same village of Akhandagarhi. When our grandfather saw that it is not possible to save himself from the Royal army, he fled to other places. At that time, there were 360 households of our family in that village. Out of all, our family members, Lala Lachman Pershad Attorney *(Mukhtaar)* and Lala Shiv Balak Lal remained in the same village in hiding. The other members of our family left that Garhi and went to places where they got shelter. For example, someone went to Dhole village, Chehra village, Saran village, Bihar, Darbhanga, Sahesram, Konki and Zamania and settled there. Our grandfather Lala Lacharam took shelter in Khasarpura located at Andhone village of Ghazipur District and settled there itself.

After overcoming that battle, our grandfather got the post of *Qanoongo* restored at Zamania Pargana and got the possession of *Zamindari* or landed property of seven villages. After that, our grandfather expired *(Baikunthbashi).* After his death, the landed property and *Zamindari* was taken over by other persons. At that time, our father and uncle both were minors. During the same period, one of our uncles by name Lala Shiv Dayal Singh who was the son of our grandfather from his first wife, had gone away towards the East which is Kanoor Dakhja. He had acquired the knowledge of witchcraft there and married a witch or sorceress. After the death of our grandfather, he came back along with that sorceress to live in the ancestral house. After a few days, that sorceress died. After her death, many evil things happened in that house. For example, rain of blood, bones etc. started.

When our grandmother saw the condition of our house, then she took our father and uncle and went to her father, Lala Roshan Lal Sahab to live there. He was the landlord of Andhone village of Ghazipur District. She started living under his patronage. She got our father and uncle educated there. Later, our father came to Banaras and initially, he was appointed to the post of *Mushrafi* and later as *Darogha* (Superintendent) of the Department of Permit, Banaras. He worked in that office for thirty years till the abolition of the department. This slave (compiler of the book) for a long period, worked in the cities of Lucknow, Calcutta, Mirzapur and other districts as Attorney (*Mukhtar*).

At present, I am staying in Hyderabad Deccan and I am in the service of Thomas Palmer Sahab Bahadur, Councillor, Hyderabad City. It may be mentioned that still there are remnants of the temple and tank and the houses constructed by the ancestors of our family in Akhanda village. Our progenitor, Lala Rekhi Raj Singh Sahab along with his younger brother, Lala Sukhi Raj Singh Sahab came down to this place (Hyderabad) from Kada (Manikpur) during the period of the kings. His progenitor was the *Qanoongo* of Zamania Pargana and Lala Sukhi Raj Sahab was appointed as the *Qanoongo* of Karanda Pargana of Ghazipur District. From that time onwards, till this time, Lala Macharam Sahab, grandfather of *Qanoongo* was living in our house. The people of our family were inhabited in Aatrol village of Zamania Pargana which is located at two *Kos* (5 Km, approximately) from Dildaar Nagar village and some other members of our family are inhabited in Mojan village of Chainpur Pargana.

Genealogical tree of Khoobchand, the compiler of this book is missing from original book.

Brief description of the family of Lala Rameshwar Dayal Sahab, son of Lala Kuldeep Chand Sahab, resident of Andhone, Ghazipur District.

The marriage of our grandfather, Lala Lacharam was celebrated with the daughter of Lala Roshan Lal. Lala Roshan Lal Sahab's family members, Nawab Rai and Rai Chandrabhan Singh reside in Revatipur, Suraj Bhan Singh in Narayanpur village. The inheritors of Lal Chand in Sherpur, the family members and the progeny of Lala Shiv Saran

Lal live in Syedpur Pargana of Ghazipur District. Their names are not known. Ram Pershad who lives in Mau village of Azamgarh and Lala Roshan Lal, employee of the godown are the noted personalities of this family. He was the Minister (Diwan) under the jurisdiction of Nawab Fazl-e-Ali Khan Sahab Bahadur for 52 years. Besides being landlord, he bought many territories and took contracts of many works. At his door, there used to be tied two chained elephants, horses, and camels. Disnath Singh worked as Tahsildar in Gorakhpur District. It is the private estate of Naval Singh, Superintendent. Bahadur Singh confined himself to his house and kept himself reciting the bhajans of Bhagwath Geeta.

The progenitors of these persons were former residents of Kada (Manikpur). This family is now residing at Akhni village and Osia village of Ghazipur District. The marriage of father of the compiler of this book, was held in the family of Lala Ram Baksh Das, resident of *Osia* and that of our uncle was celebrated in Cheenpur Pargana of Shahabad District. Both these marriages were celebrated during the lifetime of our grandfather in Zamania. It may be mentioned that Jhumakh Lal, resident of Osia and Juni Lal, resident of Kooza also belong to this family. The family tree of these persons is given next page.

Family Tree of Lala Rameshwar Dayal, son of Lala Kuldeep Chand, Lala Roshan Lal, Resident and Landlord of Andhoon village, Ghazipur District.

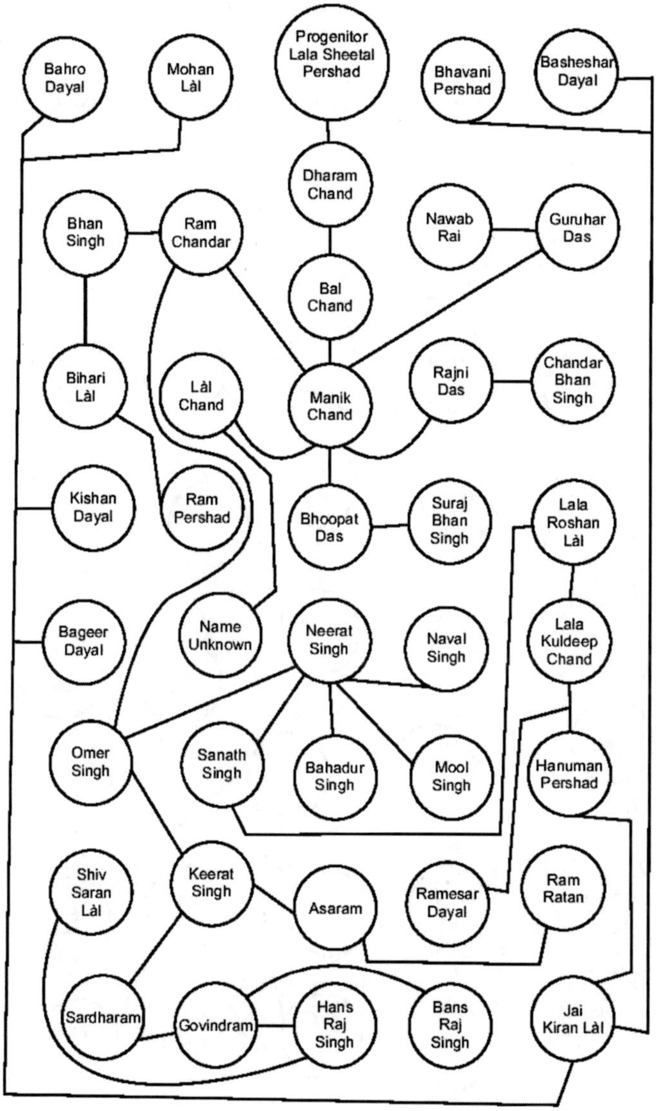

The marriage of paternal aunt *(Phoopi)* of the compiler of this book was celebrated with Rai Ram Bakhsh Singh, landlord of Khatkada, Josha Pargana of Shahabad District, and his family tree is entered below.

Family tree of Lala Dwarka Pershad and Lala Ganga Pershad.

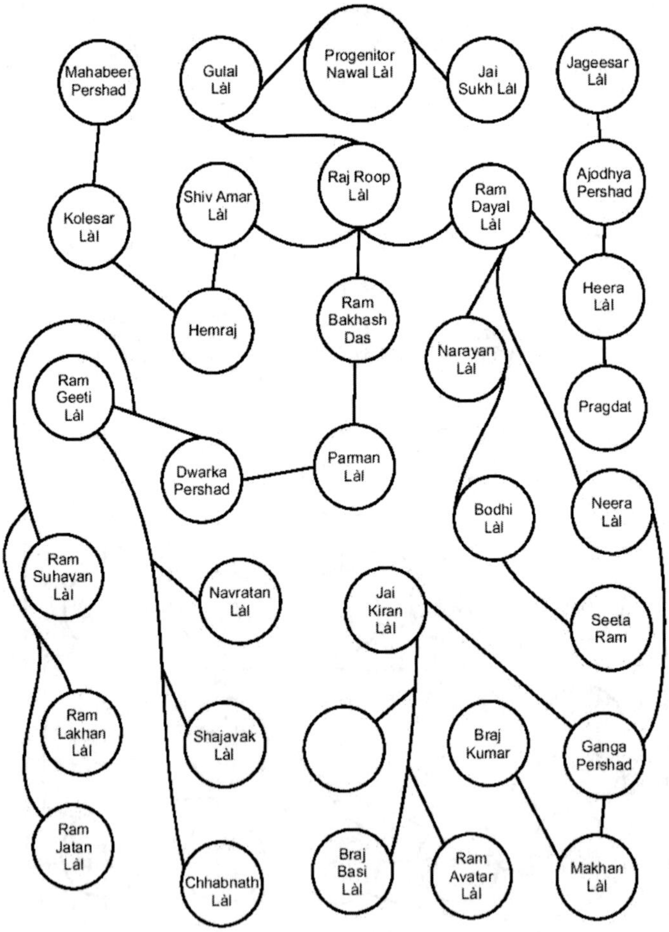

His progenitor, Rai Seetaram had adopted Bhagwat Bhajan. His son, Rai Ban Gopal Singh worked as *Qanoongo*. Ram Narayan Singh was the Minister of Raja Bagsar. He was such a wise lawyer that throughout the district, his legal ability was famous. Ram Sahi Singh was also a learned person. Due to excessive knowledge, his five senses were not intact. Rai Ram Baksh Singh had acquired a lot of property. The value of his property was about Rs 3.0 lakh. Rai Shankar Dayal was the General Attorney of Raja Bagsar. On account of his position as General Attorney, Raja Sahab Bahadur had given him *Jagir* (land given by King or Government as a reward for services).

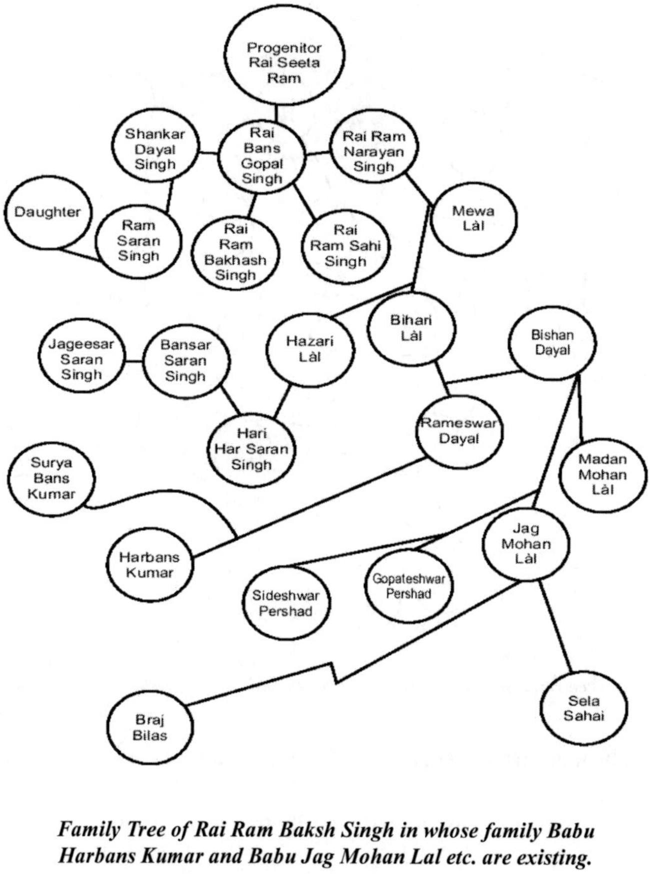

Family Tree of Rai Ram Baksh Singh in whose family Babu Harbans Kumar and Babu Jag Mohan Lal etc. are existing.

The marriage of our second paternal aunt *(Phoopi)* was celebrated with Lala Mohan Lal Sahab, resident of Cheetapur village, Ghazipur District. Munshi Debi Dayal Singh Sahab was the *Sarishtedar* in the above mentioned district and he was a very famous member of the family. His son, Munshi Sadhu Ram Sahab is also a very qualified person. He possesses an estate.

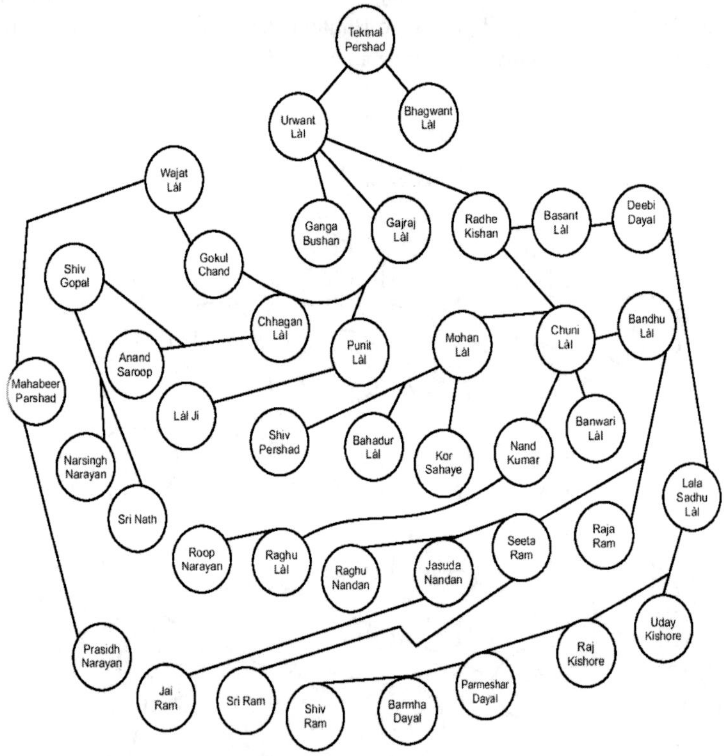

Family Tree Lala Shiv Pershad, son Mohan Lal Sahab Resident of Cheetapur.

The maternal cousin (mother's sister's son) of the compiler of this book was Lala Thakur Dayal, resident of Badoli village, Karanda Pargana, Ghazipur District. His family tree is as follows:

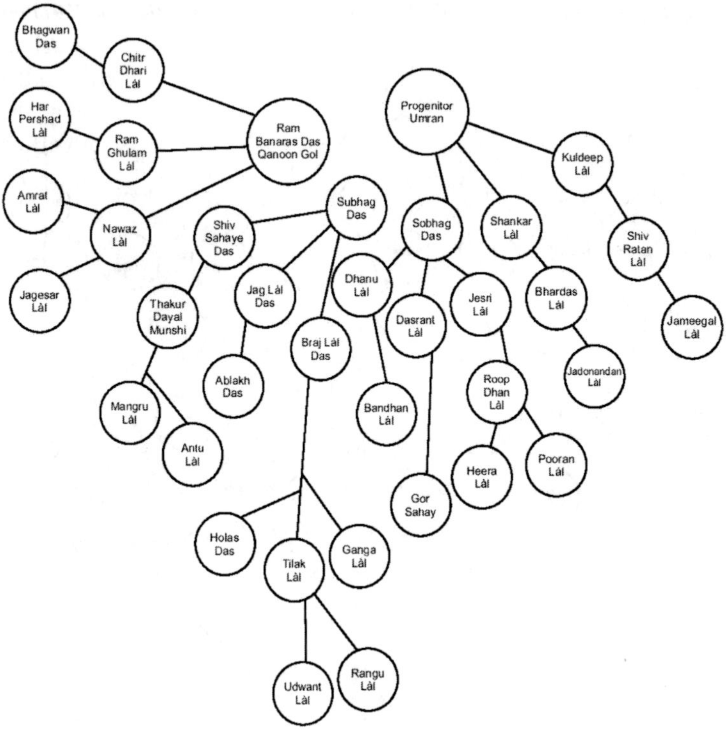

The marriage of the eldest brother of the compiler of this book, Lala Hazari Lal was celebrated with the daughter of Thakur Dayal, resident of Keetapur village, Mosi Pargana, Banaras District. He lived in this village happily. His family tree is not known. Babu Ganesh Pershad was born to my brother's first wife. When the first wife of my brother expired, he married the daughter of Thakur Dayal's second daughter. Babu Mahesh Pershad, Panna Lal, Munna Lal and Heera Lal were born to her. Panna Lal expired. All the other sons are alive.

The marriage of the younger brother of the compiler of this book, Babu Tiwari Lal was celebrated in the family of Lala Ram Charan Lal, son of Lala Budh Sen, resident of Keetapur village.

Family Tree of Lala Ram Charan Lal, son of Lala Budhsen Resident of Keetapur.

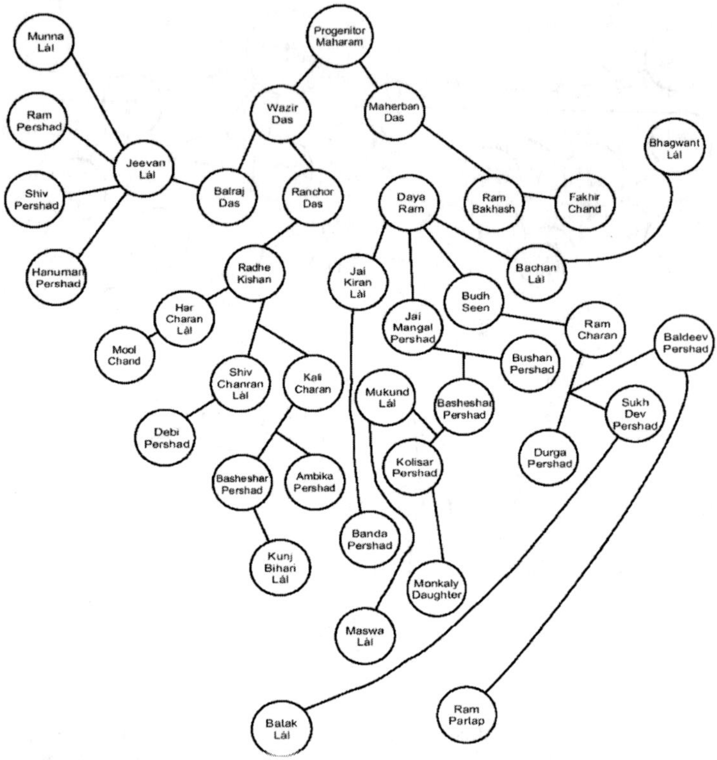

The marriage of the compiler of this book, Khoob Chand was celebrated in the family of Lala Guru Pal Singh, resident of Teewar village. The progenitors of Lala Guru Pal Singh were Shiv Das, Dhar Das, Debi Das, Devanand Das and Bhavani Das. They were inhabited in Karthima village, Kathair Pargana of Banaras District. They had many children. The progeny of one of them, Lala Bhagwan Das went to Bhagwathipur and got inhabited there. His family members are in Bhagwathipur. The progeny of another person settled down in Aasapur village of Kathair Pargana of Banaras District. His family members are still living in Aasapur. Members of this family namely; Biyayak Pershad, lawyer, son of Lala Koleshar Dayal, lawyer, and Lala Bhagwan Pershad and Lala Hanumanth Pershad, Attorneys are still alive.

Two sons of one of the progenitors namely; Lala Dileep Rai and Champat Rai got settled down in Teewar village. Shiv Baksh Rai had five sons. The eldest son, Gopal Das had a daughter who got married in the family of Lala Braj Mohan Pershad, Tahsildar, resident of Ram Nagar.

Family Tree of Lala Permeshwsar Dayal, Lala Dwaraka Pershad, Lala Bhagwant Lal, Attorneys and Lala Kasi Pershad, residents of Teewar Village, Banaras District.

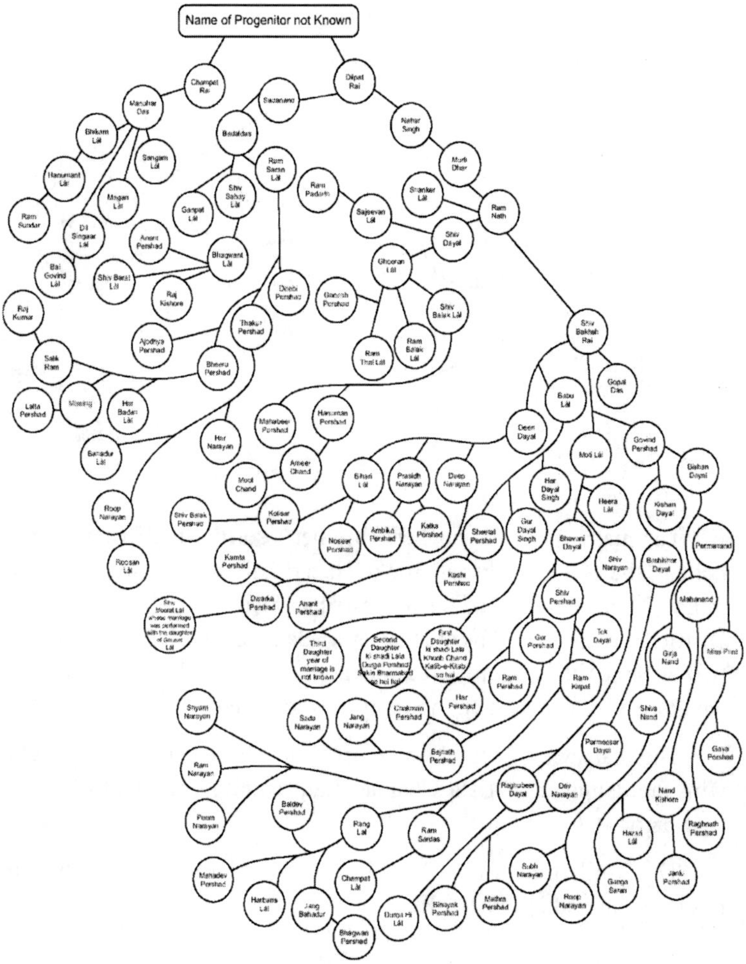

Marriage of the nephew of compiler of this book, Babu Ganesh Pershad, son of Hazari Lal was celebrated in the family of Lala Bhawani Pershad, Landlord, resident of Chetuna village, Jalhopur Pargana of Banaras District. Lala Bhawani Pershad and Babu Ganesh Pershad are alive. He is related to Sajan Lal Sahab, resident of Gast Kunda locality.

Family Tree of Lala Bhavani Pershad, resident of Chetuna Village, Jalnapur Pargana of Banaras District.

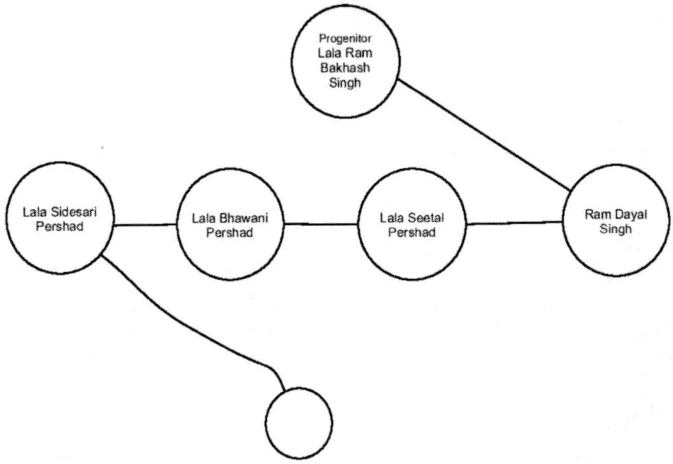

The marriage of the nephew (brother's son) of the writer of this book, Babu Mahesh Pershad, son of Hazari Lal, was held in the family of Lala Mahabeer Pershad former resident of Qaroon Village, Ghazipur District, presently residing at Jagat Gunj, Banaras City. Despite insisting two or three times, family tree was not sent. Self-addressed stamped envelope was also sent but no reply was received.

The marriage of the eldest son of Mahabeer Pershad, was held with the daughter of Lala Chaman Lal, Attorney, resident of Sarai Gowharon.

The family tree of Lala Mahabeer Pershad, whatever was known has been entered in this book.

Family Tree of Lala Mahabeer Pershad, which was known, was entered in this book.

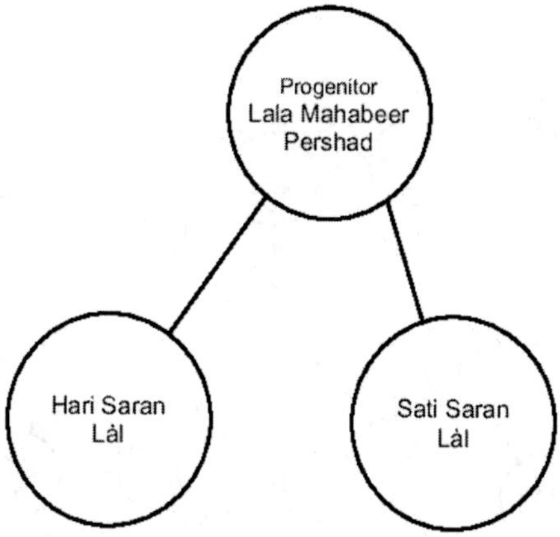

It may be noted that the wife of Babu Mahesh Pershad, daughter of Mahabeer Pershad expired in the month of June 1891 A.D. His marriage for the third time in Dubey village, Budholi Pargana in Banaras District was held in the same family.

The nephew (brother's son) of the compiler of this book, Babu Mahesh Pershad, married in the family of Lala Ram Lotan Lal Sahab, resident of Shahabuddinpur, Karakat Town of Jonepur District. Lala Gaya Pershad is his uncle (meaning *Qaloo* that is mother's sister's husband). He lives in Baliya. Besides them, in this family, Munshi Hegan Lal Sahab was Deputy Collector, whose son; Munshi Kishan Sahab is the landlord and resident of Karakat. He is a very polite person. He was the cherisher of his brothers and affable to them.

The marriage of the brother's son of the compiler of this book Babu Munna Lal, son of my brother Hazari Lal was celebrated in the family of Man Mohan Lal Sahab, resident of Gangapur, Kiswar Taluka pertaining to the estate of Maharaja of Banaras. The family tree of Lala Man Mohan Lal Sahab is this.

His progenitor was Diwan of Maharaja Balwant Singh, son of Jawahar Lal, Deewan of Raja Naroda Narayan Singh Bahadur, Mau Gunj state of Raj Uwan.

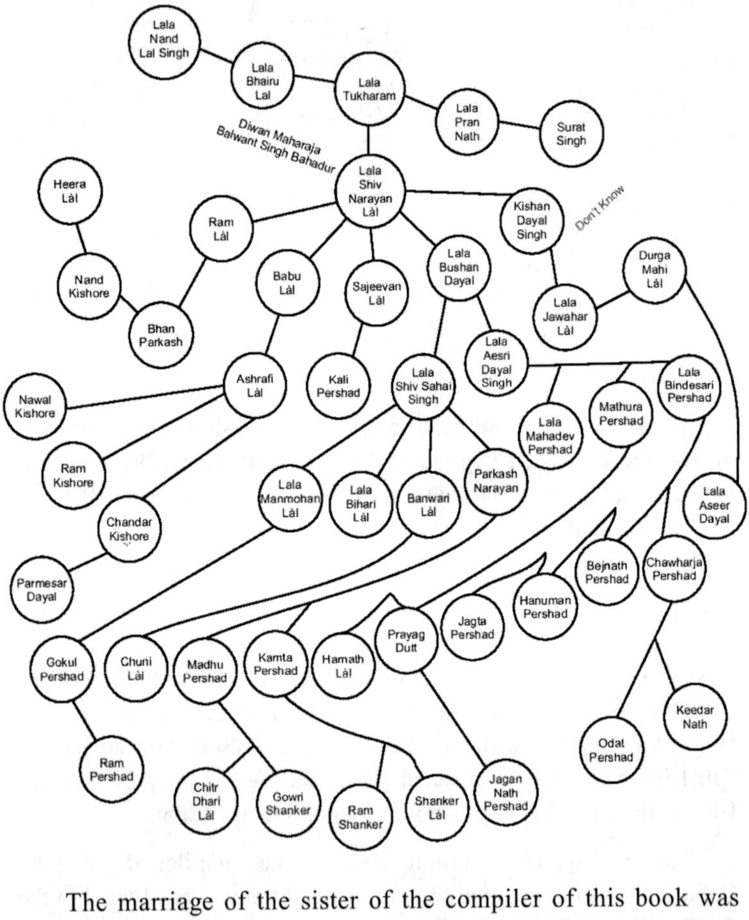

The marriage of the sister of the compiler of this book was celebrated with Lala Bahadur Lal, brother of Lala Jagannath Pershad, Braj Mohan Pershad and Ajodhya Pershad, residents of Ram Nagar, Banaras District. His family tree is not known. Whatever is known is entered below:

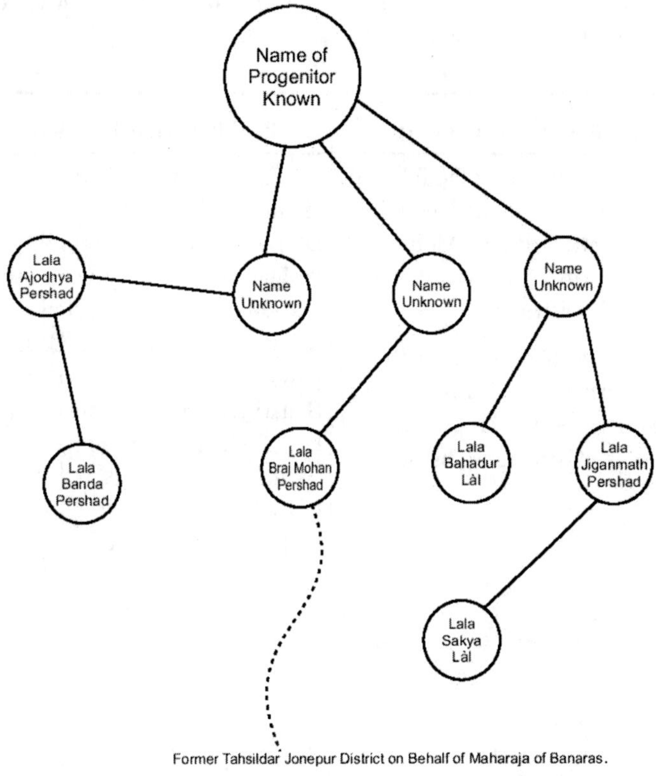

The marriage of the nephew (brother's son) of the compiler of this book, Babu Heera Lal was celebrated in the year 1890 in the family of Lala Har Narayan Lal Sahab, employee of Maharaja of Banaras, resident of Kesupur village, Budhol Pargana of Banaras District. In the village mentioned above, there are many members of the community. All of them are very polite, educated and belong to esteemed families. Despite demand, the family tree was not received.

Brethren living in the city of Banaras with whom dining and drinking relations are in vogue

<table>
<tr><th>Prahlad Ghat Locality</th><th>Prahlad Ghat Locality</th></tr>
<tr><td>

The marriage of the father of Lala Ganesh Pershad was held with the sister of Lala Mohan Lal, resident of Cheetapur Village, Ghazipur District.

Lala Mahabeer Pershad son of Lala Kishan Pershad Sahab is at present Deputy Inspector of Schools of Mirzapur District.

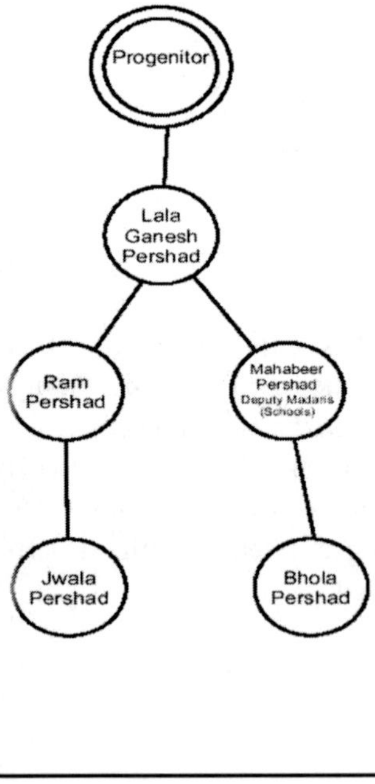

</td><td>

Lala Kuldeep Chand Sahab, resident of Peetapur, Ghazipur District, presently residing at Prahlad Ghat locality, whose sons are Lala Jawahar Lal, Peshkaar (Office Assistant in the Court of Law) in Ghazipur District and Lala Behari Lal, Deputy Collector and Lala Gajadhar Pershad Sahab.

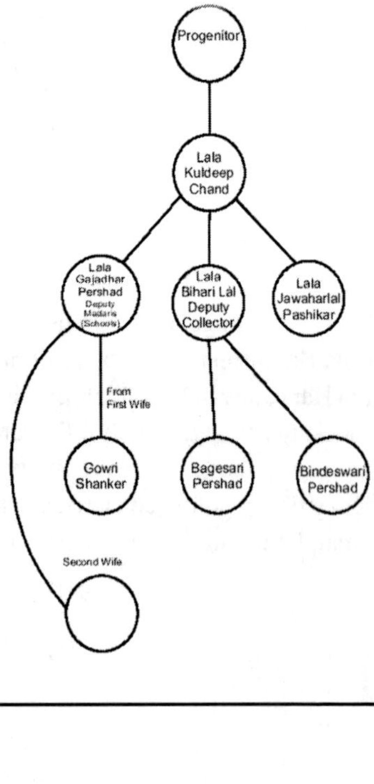

</td></tr>
</table>

Teeliya Nala Locality	Delhi Bazar Locality
Lala Lajpat Sahab Lala Janaki Pershad Sahab Lala Kasicharan Lal Sahab Jogesh Pershad Sahab	Lala Bhagwant Lal Sahab, Attorney–office of the Commissioner, resident of Teewar. Lala Ram Pershad and Lala Shiv Pershad Attorneys, residents of Teewar. Lala Tulsi Pershad Saheb, resident of Teewar. Lala Jawahar Lal Saheb – Court Officer (Sarishtedar)

<table>
<tr><th>Jagat Gunj Locality</th><th>Begesari Debi Locality</th></tr>
<tr><td>Lala Mahabeer Pershad Sahab –resident of Qaroon.</td><td rowspan="3">Lala Ganesh Pershad Sahab, Former Inspector (Naazir) of Criminal Court.

Lala Jawahar Lal Sahab - Lala Beechu Lal Sahab, son of Lala Thakur Dayal Sahab, former resident of Miyan Ki Mandi, presently residing at Kabeer Chowraha, whose marriage was held in the family of Lala Braj Mohan Pershad, resident of Ram Nagar, in his family women are existing now.

Munshi Binayak Pershad, Advocate of the Court.</td></tr>
<tr><th>Kabeer Chowraha Locality</th></tr>
<tr><td>Munshi Raj Kumar Sahab, former Court officer (Sarishtedar) of Criminal Court, Banaras.

Lala Sheetal Pershad Sahab – whose relationship is with Lala Braj Mohan Pershad and Lala Jigannath Pershad, Ajodhya Pershad, residents of Ram Nagar and he is the relative of Lala Raghuvbansh Sahay.

Lala Bhagwan Pershad, Attorney.

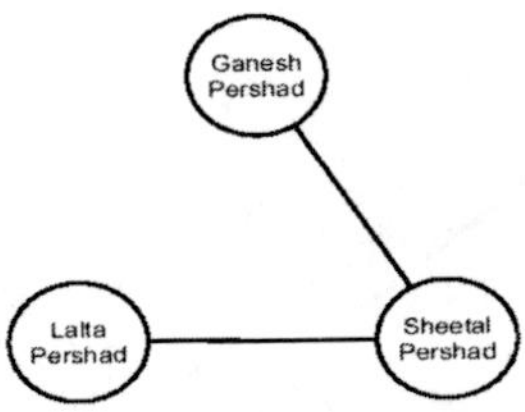</td></tr>
</table>

Wasan Gunj Locality	Agast Kunda Locality
Lala Bindeswari Pershad, Deputy Collector.	Lala Lachman Lal Saheb, who is related to Lala Bhawani Pershad, resident of Chetunasi.
Raja Darwaza Locality	**Chandan Shaheed Locality**
Munshi Shiv Sahay Singh Sahab, former Administrator *(Munsarim),* Estate of Raja Jonepur, whose son, Munshi Mahadev Pershad Saheb is the Deputy Inspector of Schools.	Lala Debi Pershad Sahab, who is related to Lala Parmeshwar Dayal, resident of Teewar.
	Kabeer Chowraha Locality
	Munshi Gahwarleet Lal Sahab, General Attorney of Raja Korak whose family tree is separate.

Family Tree of the Progenitor of Lala Anant Pershad

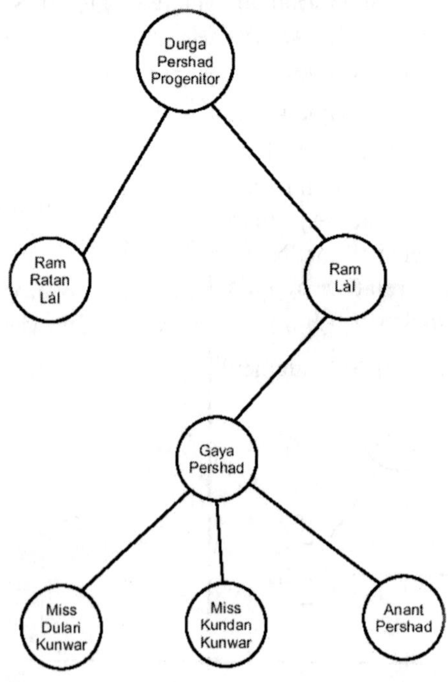

Family Tree of Lala Mahaveer Pershad Sahab Resident of Qazi Sandosi locality

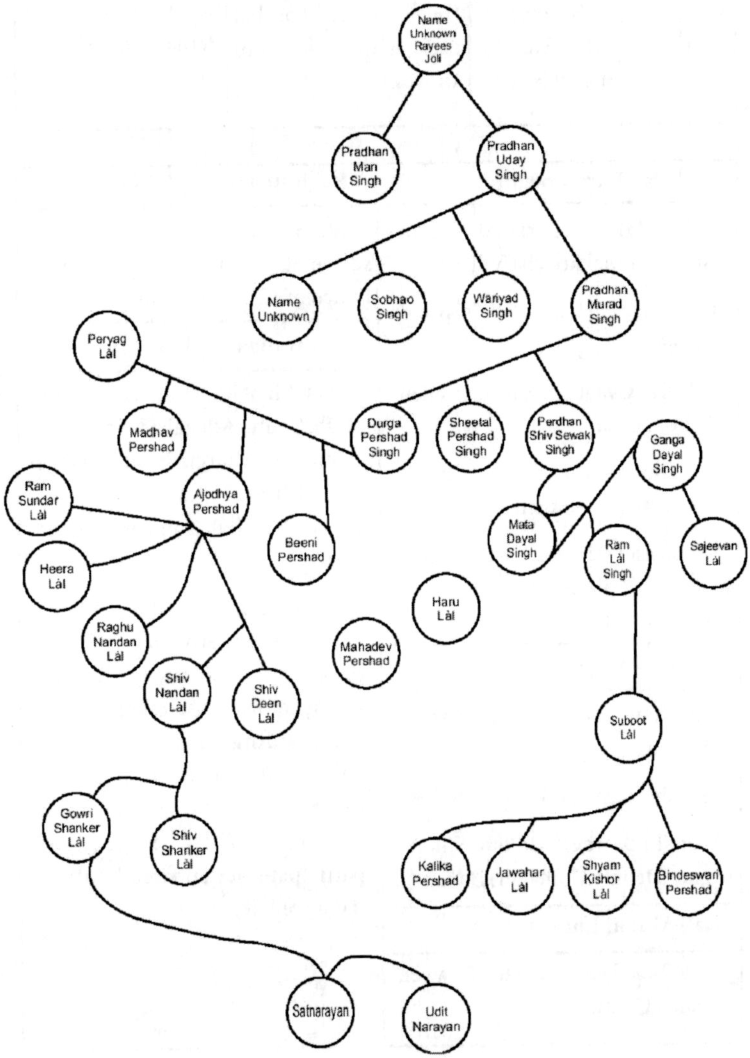

The progeny of these persons is in Parpetpur Village, Mandiya Havan Paragana, Jonepur Distric and in Khokhtair Village, Badohi Paragana, Mirzapur District.

Qazi Sandosi Locality	HouzKatora Locality	Alipura Locality
Lala Banwari Lal Sahab, Lala Munnalal Saheb, son of Kanhaiyalal Sahab, Lala Taik Pershad Sahab	Lala Sunkta Pershad. He has three sons but their names are not known.	Lala Thakur Dayal Sahab Lala Mahadev Perhad Sahab

Vilay Pare Locality
Lala Mahesh Pershad Sahab, resident of Mahkoocha Village. Lala Sajeevan Lal Sahab, Inspector *(Daroga)*. Lala Bhagwant Lal Sahab, resident of Mashoocha. Munshi Raijhal Singh Sahab, Former Judge (Munsiff). Lala Kashi Pershad Sahab, who is related to Lala Bhawani Pershad, resident of Chetuna.

Dara Nagar Locality
Lala Ram Pratap Sahab, former Tahsildar. Munshi Lachman Pershad Sahab. Munshi Baldev Baksh Sahab, former Deputy Collector, Banaras.

Kali Mahal Locality
Lala Taik Dayal Sahab, Lawyer, Banaras Court.

Bagh Bedar Singh Locality
Lala Sukhlal Singh Sahab whose son is at present Commissioner of Police of Kumb Banaras.

Aurangabad Locality
Lala Man Rai Sahab, Lawyer, High Court, Allahabad, in whose family are Munshi Jwala Pershad and Munshi Lalta Pershad, Lawyers of High Court, mentioned above. It may be mentioned that among the brethren of Srivastav, residents of Banaras, it is a tradition *(Dastur)* in vogue that those relatives who are residing in nearby areas, participate in the dining and drinking parties and in major functions. All the relations participate but apparently all of them are one.

Brethren of Srivastav residents and the nobles of Bahadurpur village of Banaras District

Lala Fakhir Chand Sahab

Lala Gowrilal Sahab

Lala Hazari Lal Sahab

Lala Banwari Lal Sahab

Lala Raj Narayan Sahab

Lala Mukhchid Lal Sahab

Lala Braj Mohan Lal Sahab

Lala Ramesar Dayal Sahab

Lala Sunkta Pershad Sahab

Lala Mahabeer Pershad Sahab

Brethren of Srivastav *Khaas* residents of Dildar Nagar village, Zamania Pargana, Ghazipur District

Lala Chote Lal Mahesh Pershad Sahab, resident of Zamania.

Lala Lachuman Pershad Sahab, Attorney and Shiv Balak Lal Sahab, resident of Dildar Nagar.

Brethren of Srivastav Cheenpur Pargana of Shahabad District

Lala Amrut Lal Sahab, resident of Kanki, Sahesram Pargana.

Lala Siv Sahay Singh Sahab, resident of Ghehwan.

Lala Sajan Lal Sahab, resident of Batoyi.

Another noble and rich man of Budhan village but his name is not known. We have relationship with him and Lala Ram Baksh, resident of Khatkhara is also related.

Brethren of Srivastav community of Jonepur District

Lala Ambika Pershad, son of Munshi Gur Pershad Sahab (late), resident of Bhagwatipur.

Lala Hardev Sahab, resident of Bhotipur, employee of Ghalib Jung Bahadur.

Brethren of Srivastav community of Mirzapur city

Lala Paragdeb Sahab, Attorney *(Mukhtaar)* in Collectorate, Mirzapur.

Lala Babu Lal Sahab whose relationship is with the family of Lala Kalicharan Lal.

Lala Ram Lal Sahab.

Lala Babu Lal Sahab, Lawyer, who is related to Ghorset Lal Sahab.

Lala Mahadev Pershad Sahab.

Lala Beeni Pershad Sahab son of Jasoomanand Sahab.

Lala Munna Lal Sahab, Lawyer, High Court.

I (the compiler of the book) met this person at Manmad Railway Station. He accompanied me to Hyderabad and stayed with us. We tried our best for his employment. We have relationship with him and Gahwarleet Lal.

Raja Jalpa Pershad whose Family Tree is entered below

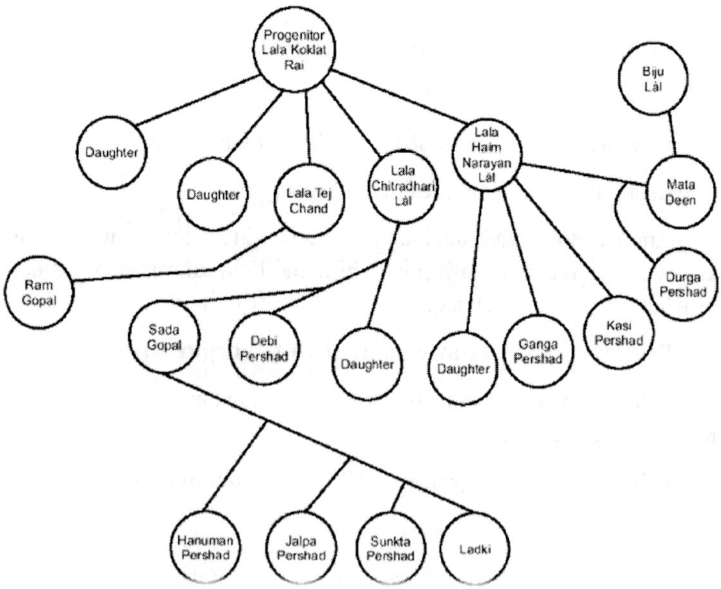

Brethren of Srivastav community of Sahabad District

Babu Harish Kumar, Babu Madan Mohan Lal, Babu Jagmohan Lal, residents and landlords of Khatkhara village, Chousa Pargana whose family tree is entered separately.

Babu Durga Pershad Sahab is the resident of the above mentioned village. His father Devaki Nandan Lal Singh Sahab (late) was a very generous person. Whosoever approached him was not deprived of his bounty. His family tree is as follows:

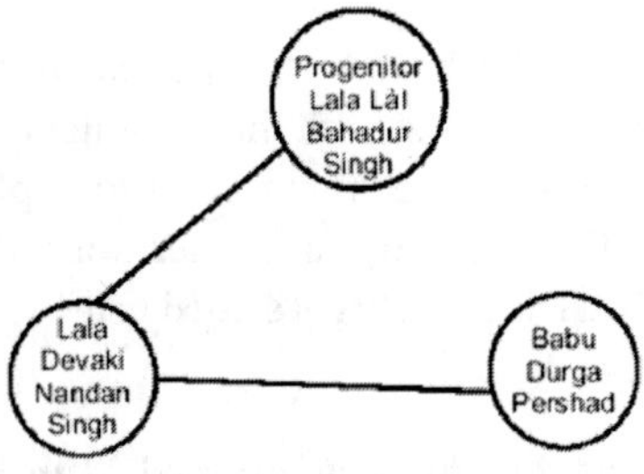

Lala Doman Lal Sahab, resident of Khatkara village, Chousa Pargana. His Family Tree is as follows

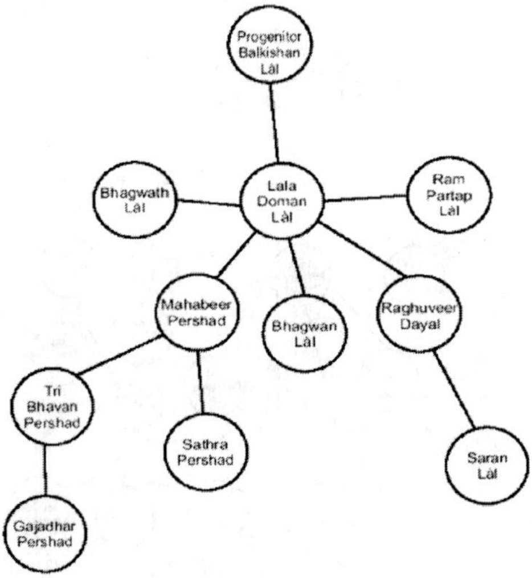

Munshi Sahab Ram Sahab, lawyer, resident of Chousa Khaas was a very polite person. He cherished his brothers. Despite demand, his family tree was not received.

Lala Ramanand Sahab, son of Sachdanand Sahab, resident of Khatkhara was asked to give his family tree but he did not give.

Munshi Sathra Pershad, Court Officer *(Peshkar)* of the Criminal Court behaves very politely with his brothers. Their ancestors were *Diwan* (Minister) and *Bakhshis* (paymasters of the army) of Raja Bagsar previously. The family tree was demanded through Munshi Dwaraka Pershad but it was not given.

Munshi Dwaraka Pershad, Attorney (*Mukhtaar*) of the Criminal Court of Bagsar is very polite with the community and his ancestors place is Marha. He has been living at various places and reached Sesondha village, Chousa Pargana, the territory of Tribhuvan Singh resident of Shahabad District. He got settled in the village of this district and also in Baliya district.

The family Tree of the above-mentioned Munshi Sahab is given below

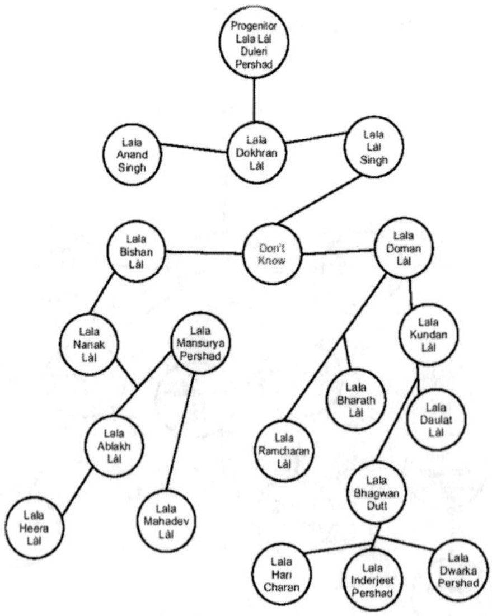

Goud brothers and Bhatnagar brothers at Banaras.

Goud Brothers residents of Prahlad Ghat	Bhatnagar Brothers residents of Taliya Nala adjacent to Tilochan Locality
Baldev Singh Dayal Sahab Munshi Ram Pershad (Late), Lawyer. Munshi Gunwan Lal Sahab (Late) whose grandson is Lala Hanuman Pershad.	Munshi Har Pershad Sahab (Late) whose grandson (daughter's son) is Lala Purshotam Lal Sahab. Munshi Ram Pershad Sahab. Munshi Batchu Singh Sahab whose son is Lala Khor Sen, Lawyer at Small Causes Court of Hyderabad. Lala Sohan Lal Sahab Lala Debi Pershad Sahab Munshi Nand Kishore Sahab, former Inspector of Customs (Girdavar, Chungi) Munshi Seetaram Sahab, Deputy Collector. Lala Ladli Pershad Sahab Lala Lalta Pershad Sahab Lala Babbu Singh Sahab Lala Shyam Sundar Lal Sahab Lala Jagdish Pershad Sahab

It may be noted that all the above mentioned persons are well-to-do people. All of them are so competent *(Laiq)* that if anyone tests them in any work, they participate in that work presuming it as their work.

This humble servant *(Banda)* Khoobchand and Munshi Gahwarleet Lal Sahab, former resident of Aasthan Zafarabad, Jonepur District, presently residing at Kabeer Chowraha, Banaras City have relationship and brotherhood. At present, he has come to Hyderabad Deccan along with Maharaja Sahab Bahadur Kirk. The compiler of this book told Munshi Sahab to get the family tree of his relatives since the said Munshi Sahab himself wrote down his family tree and the family tree of his relatives and gave it to me with appreciation for myself. Although the writer of this book does not deserve this appraisal but if I had not written it, Munshi Sahab, in his heart would have felt unhappy. It was therefore, thought it appropriate to enter this appraisal as it is in this book which is as follows:

Since Munshi Khoobchand, former resident of Zamania, Ghazipur District presently staying at Prahalad Ghat, Banaras City, Territory of Thomas Palmer Sahab, Barrister, is such a polite person cherishing his brothers that whosoever belonging to the community and brotherhood comes to Hyderabad from India (meaning North India) for employment or for any other need or purpose, he expresses concern for him, helps him with the money needed and recommends. So long as he won't get his need fulfilled, he spends money from his pocket for his food etc. He also helps him to the extent possible for his stay and food. If there is no opportunity to get his work done, he arranges to send him to India (meaning North India). During this period, one or two persons came to him and borrowed money from him to the extent of Rs 200-400 and fled. Even I was not feeling comfortable in Hyderabad, although this city is magnificent and elegant. From the time I met Munshi Sahab, I am satisfied. Whenever, I get worried, I enjoy the company of Munshi Sahab.

Munshi Sahab was preparing the family trees of his family and other relatives himself. He asked me to get my family tree immediately. Accordingly to the wish of Munshi Sahab, I sought the family trees of each and every one of my relatives and gave them to him. A few days back, the family tree of the family residing at Zafarabad was received, due to the attention paid by Munshi Umaan Pershad. Our ancestors had occupied for several generations, the post of Minister during the Royal period at the capital of the country, Shahjehanpur which is called Delhi.

Baba Shiv Bans Singh who was our progenitor also occupied the post of minister. Later, due to the wrath of the king of the time, he relinquished the said post and from Teetagarh, he went to eastern side along with God's idol and *Purohit* (family priest) and Barber. He came down to Nawada village, Gonda taluka of Jonepur District. He settled there. At that place, there still exists a temple and God's idol. After a few days stay, he got the position of *Qanoongo* (Revenue functionary) of Biyasi and Zafarabad Parganas. In addition to these villages, he got Sanghipur chek Mahmood and Nankari villages for collecting revenues. In this way, he settled down in Sanghipur village of Nankari area. Later, he selected Saknipur and settled down in Makhdoompur, Zafarabad taluka of Jonepur District. He is still continuing the *Zamindari* of Saknipur. Chek Mahmood village is still in the possession of our family members, as per the previous tradition.

In Sankipur village *Shivalaya* (Shiva's temple) and *Dharamshala* were constructed by our ancestors which still exist. Our people constructed garden etc. there. From the earlier days, this family is famous as *"Barah Ghar"*. The position of *Qanoongoyi* is still continuing in our family right from the days of royalty. Baba Ram Bakhsh Singh, Meherban Singh, Lala Hazari Lal, Lala Durga Pershad Sahab, Lala Heet Lal Sahab, Lala Shivan Lal Sahab, Lala Kalika Pershad Sahab were from our family who were functioning as *Qanoongos* (revenue collecting officials). My sons, Lala Kalika Pershad Sahab and Lala Baldev Pershad are working as *Qanoongo*.

The position of *Qanoongo* is still continuing in our family from generation to generation. Our paternal forefather, Lala Nand Kumar Lal Sahab, was the Lawyer at Banaras Court. After his death, our uncle (Umomi) Lala Salik Ram Sahab became the lawyer in the Law Court of Banaras. After three years he expired in Banaras. He was a very senior lawyer. Our cousin (Paternal uncle's son) Munshi Gowri Shankar Lal Sahab was a very competent and knowledgeable person. He expired during the life time of our uncle. Our father, functioned as Munshi in the Criminal Court of Banaras till the tenure of Zamin Khan Sahab and then resigned. Later, he was appointed as Court of Wards of Raja Shiv Lal Dubey, Raja of Jonepur. He continued in that position till the abolition of Court of Wards. When Raja Lachmi Narayan expired, he relinquished the job.

Our paternal uncle, Munshi Prasanna Lal Sahab was also a Grade –I officer of the Collectorate of Banaras. It is now six years that he expired. He was very competent *Munshi* (Clerk). Now my cousin (my paternal uncle's son) Ram Swaroop is alive.

This servant (the compiler of the book) is at present working as *Munshi* (clerk) and General Attorney of Maharaja Bahadur. Maharaja Somasekhar Rajender, Minister Bahadur of Maharaja Coorg and the younger brother Babu Jawahar Lal, General Attorney of Honourable Raja Shiv Pershad Sahab "Sitara Hind".

It may be mentioned that the family tree could not be read clearly. It was known to the extent that Lala Deep Chand, Uttam Chand, Kasinath Singh, Unath Singh, the family of Baba Soban Das Singh, progenitor, according to a decision, went to the South and got settled there. Lala Manik Chand Sahab also went towards Southern side. He lives there, but we are not aware of him. Lala Beechak Lal Singh along with family went to Devarda village in Jonepur District and settled there. At present, the family of Munshi Bansi Pershad Sahab along with his brothers and other members is in Miyanpur locality of Ghazipur City. Munshi Besi Pershad Sahab, till this date was Security Officer (*Muhafiz*) in Collectorate of Ghazipur District and Tehsildar of Syedpur Pargana. He died in Banaras City. The family of Munshi Sahab still lives in Miyanpur locality of Ghazipur city. Lala Banwari Lal Sahab, brother of Lala Sathura Pershad Sahab is the nephew (brother's son) of the late Munshi Sahab. In our 12th house meaning from all the people are still continuing the tradition. There is no animosity or displeasure among them so far. They have hereditary territories together. Besides this family, two more families which are related, have been living in Hyderabad for several generations. Their attitude is brotherly as mentioned above, but they do not have any share in the hereditary property. It may be mentioned that near Zafarabad, there is a village called Lachman Tela, where there are houses of two or three Kayasths but from the ancient times, we have no tradition of dining and drinking with them. We do not have any contact with these persons also. Here is the family tree of Ghorset Lal and his relatives, residents of Zafarabad, Jonepur District, presently residing at Kabeer Chowraha, Banaras City.

Family tree of the relatives who have been living in Zafarabad for the past many generations

Family Tree of Lala Ajodhya Pershad Sahab, who is one of the relatives and he is one of the progenitors but from the previous family tree, it is not known who are his relatives and what is their relationship.

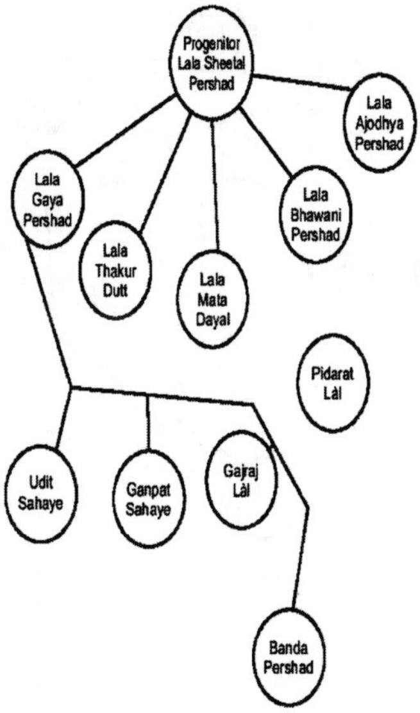

Family Tree of Munshi Uman Pershad Sahab, whose grandfather was Lala Ram Bakhsh Singh Sahab. His marriage was held with the sister of Lala Shiv Deen Lal Sahab, *Qanoongo*. Lala Sahab was the noble (*Rayees*) of Mah Koocha, Gurdara Pargana, Jonepur District. At present, the family is living in Zafarabad due to relationship.

Family Tree of Munshi Sahab is entered below.

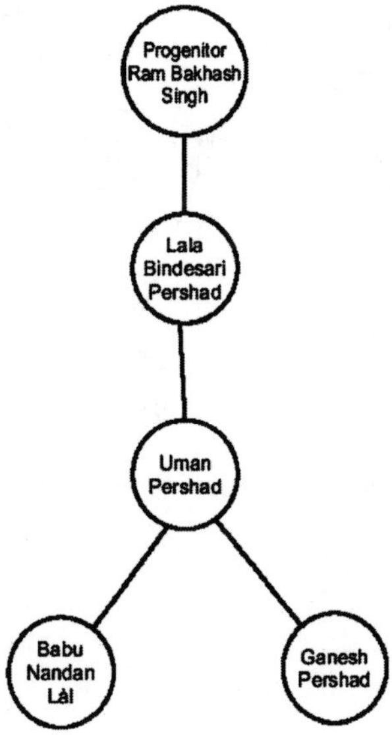

Our great grandfather's father Lala Rang Lal's marriage was held in the family of Lala Ojha Mal Sahab at Konera, Machli Shehar Taluka of Jonepur District. The family tree is not fully known. Whatever has been written is entered here.

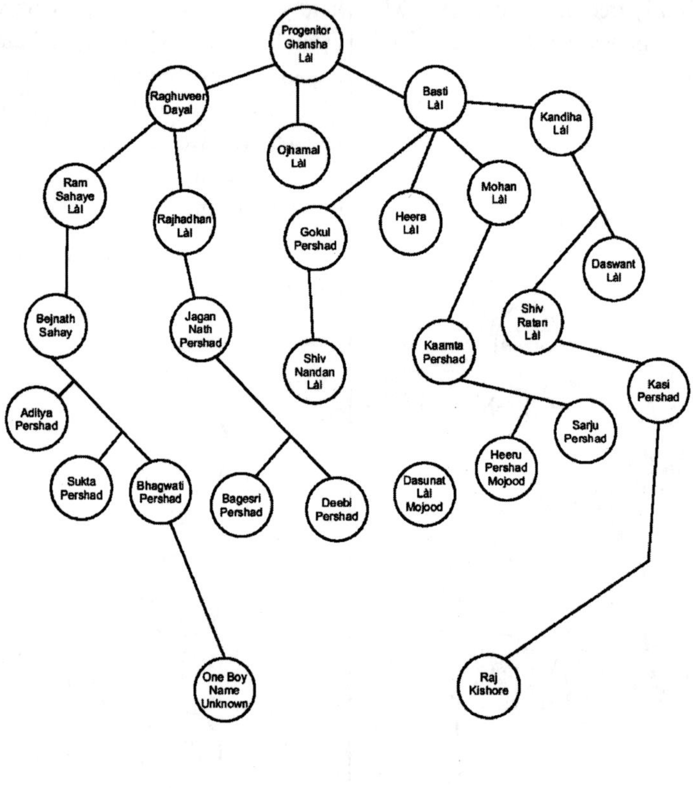

The first marriage of grandfather, Nand Kumar Singh was held in the family of Lala Sri Kishan Lal Sahab. Lala Sri Kishan Lal Sahab was the resident of Aasapur village of Jonepur District, presently residing at Kabeerpura Chowraha, Banaras City. He was the cousin (mother's brother's son of our father). His family tree is as follows.

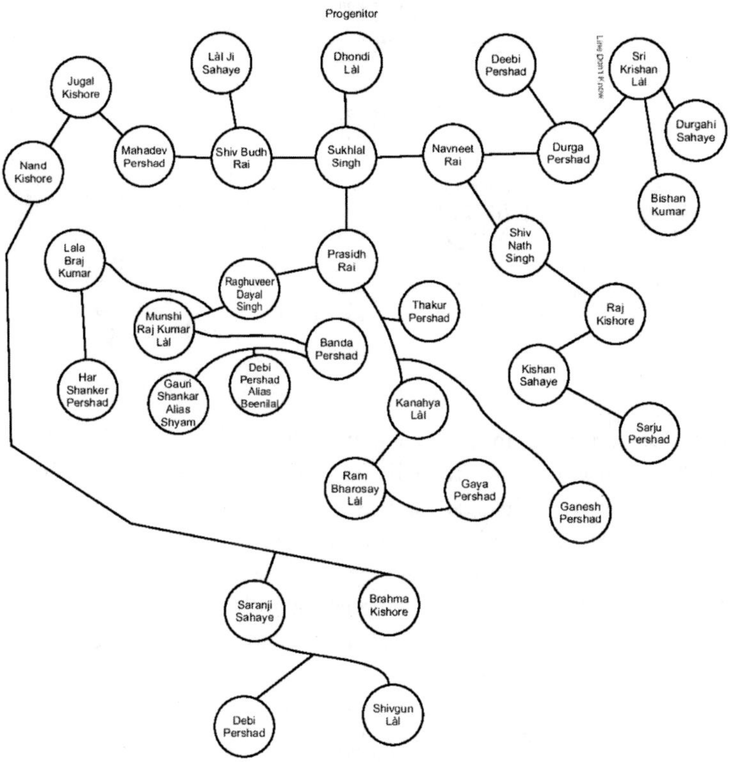

Our second grandfather, Lala Nand Kumar Singh Sahab, resident of Rohata, Jonepur city married the daughter of Lala Kanahya Lal. Family Tree of Lala Kanahya Lal (Late) is as follows:

Progenitor

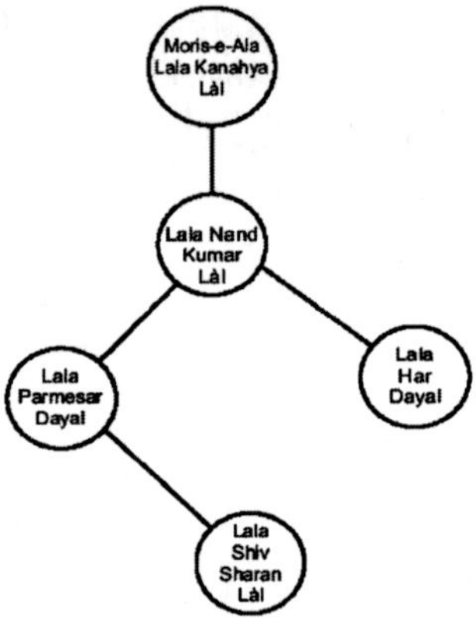

The marriage of my paternal grandfather, Lala Bhiku Lal was held in Chiryakot village of Azamgarh District. The brother of my paternal grandmother, Lala Shankar Lal was a lawyer. He was living with his family at Peeri Kalaan locality of Banaras City. Since the family tree was not known completely, it has been entered according to memory. His son is Lala Shankar Lal. There are other sons also whose names are not known. There are sons of Lala Shankar Lal whose names are not known to people. The family tree of Lala Shankar Lal (late) is as follows.

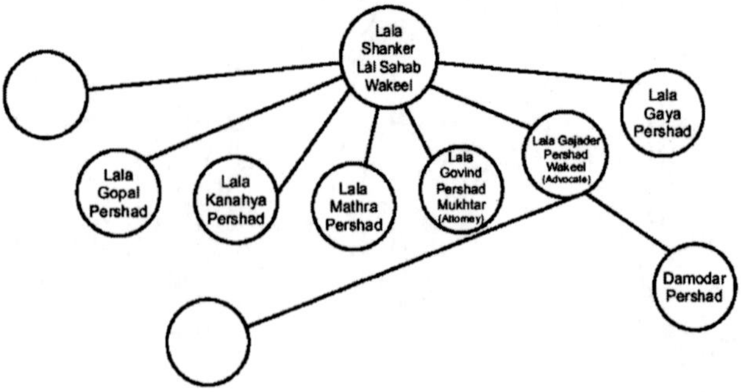

The first marriage of our uncle (father's brother), Lala Salik Ram, resident of Bandari locality, Jonepur city was held in the family of Lala Dusa Ram and the second marriage was held in the family of Lala Ram Paltan Lal Sahab, resident of Paan Dareba locality of Jonepur city. In both these families, no one is alive now.

The family tree of Lala Dusa Ram is entered here

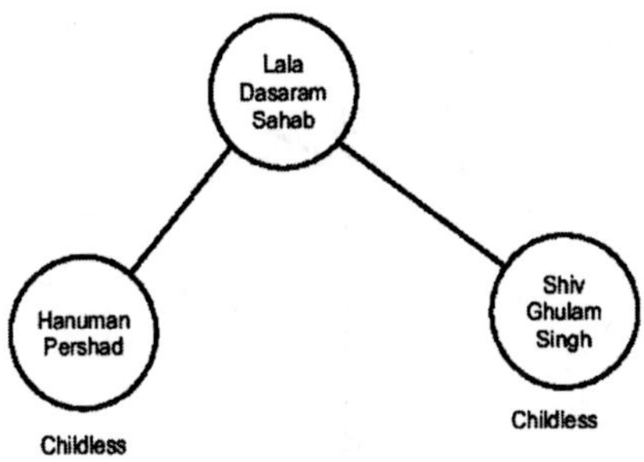

The maternal relatives of the compiler of this book are from Kota village, Devgaon pargana of Azamgarh. There is no one in this family now. Janab Ajodhya Pershad Sahab was our maternal grandfather and Lala Mahabeer Pershad was his brother. These persons were employed at Saugar. In this place, there is a temple of Sri Maha Rani Palnaji Devi. Due to this, my mother named my son Babu Palna Pershad after this Goddess. The family tree of my maternal grandfather Ajodhay Pershad is entered here.

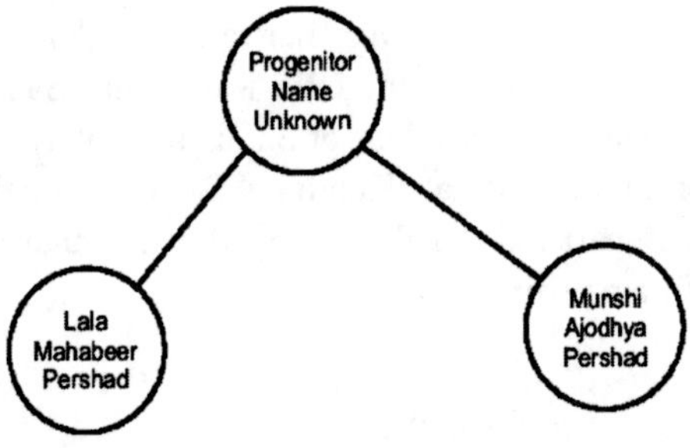

The marriage of our uncle (father's brother), Lala Pershan Lal Sahab was held in the family of Lala Radhe Kishan Lal Sahab, resident of Sipah locality of Jonepur city. There is no one in this family now.

Here is the family tree

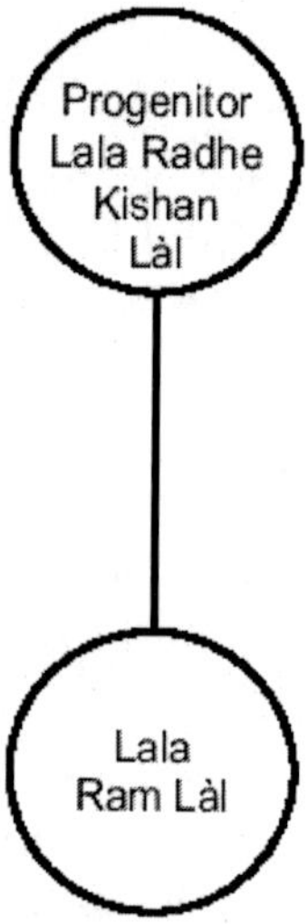

The marriage of our first paternal aunt (father's sister) was held with Munshi Durga Pershad Sahab, resident of Rampur village, Mandiya Hone Pargana of Jonepur District. Lala Sahab mentioned above is from the family of Kanavan village of the said district. The marriage of the daughter of Lala Banwari Lal Sahab was held with my cousin (father's sister's son) Lala Ramanand Sahab, son of Lala Gambheer Lala Sahab resident of Sarai Barkho. The marriage of my nephew (brother's son) Lala Kundi Lal Sahab, was held with the sister of Munshi Behari Lal Sahab, son of Munshi Janaki Pershad Sahab, resident of Paranwan.

The Family Tree of paternal uncle (father's sister's husband) Durga Pershad, resident of Rampur Village Mandiya Hone Pargana, Jonepur District is entered here

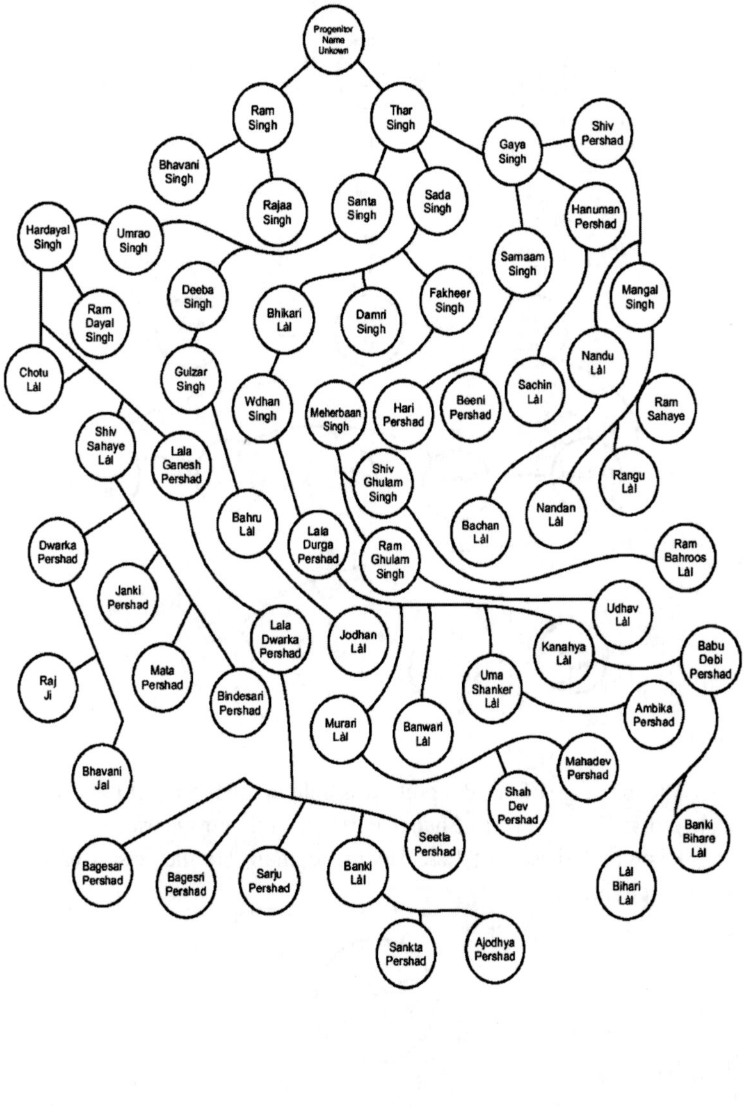

The marriage of our second paternal aunt (father's sister) was held with Munshi Ajodhya Pershad, resident of Khatavan village, Mandiya Hone Pargana, Jonepur District. His family is very famous and renowned.

The family tree is as follows:

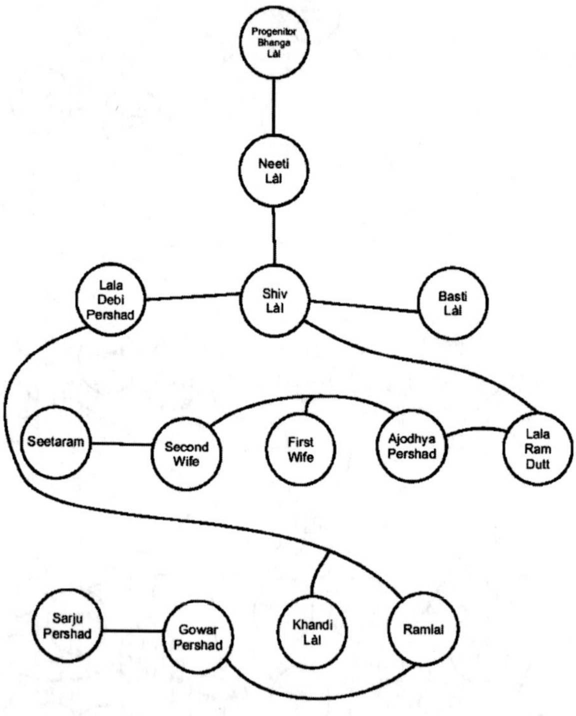

The marriage of one daughter was held in the family of Lala Beeni Pershad at Gora, Machili Sheher Pargana, Jonepur District with Lala Raj Kishore Lal, son of Lala Beeni Pershad. He has a son named Ghanpat Sahaye.

Our paternal cousin (father's brother's son) Lala Gowri Shankar Lal's marriage was held in the family of Lala Ganga Pershad and Sheetal Pershad and Mata Pershad at Hari Patti village, Maduheen Pargana, Mirzapur District. The progeny of Lala Gur Pershad and Lala Hanuman Pershad and the late two brothers-in-law and their progeny is existing. It may be mentioned that Lala Gur Pershad Sahab has relationship in Mirzapur with Munshi Babu Lal Sahab, father-in-law of my son, Babu Palna Pershad. The compiler of this book personally got the family tree written by going to Mirzapur.

Family Tree of Lala Gur Pershad, resident of Hari Patti village, Maduhin Pargana, former resident of Tola Chak village, Banaras District

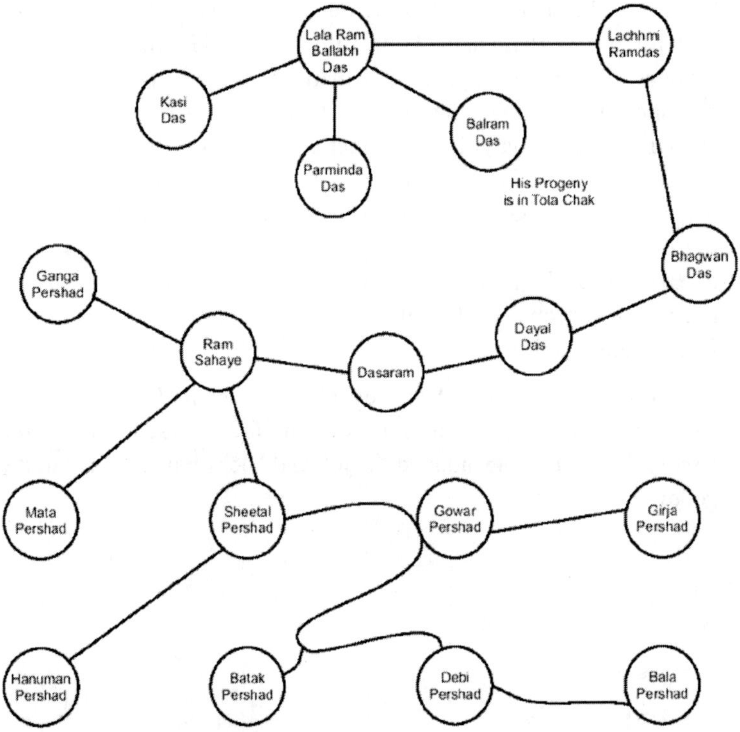

The marriage of our second paternal cousin (father's brother's son) Munshi Bachu Lal Sahab was held in Kajagaon alias Syed Gaon, Jonepur District, in the family of Lala Himmat Lal Sahab, Minister *(Deewan)*.Now only the brother-in-law of Lala Gur Dayal Lal Sahib exists. Lala Gur Dayal Lal Sahab has a daughter whose marriage has been held in Sipah locality of Jonepur city. Family tree was not received from them.

The marriage of the sister of the compiler of this book was held with Munshi Mata Badal Lal Sahab, resident of Sarai Harkho, Jonepur District and the marriage of father of Munshi Mata Badal Sahab was held with the sister of Munshi Ganpat Dayal Bakshi and the marriage of the sister of Mata Badal Lal was held at Handiya, Allahabad District with Lala Jarbandhan Lal, younger brother of Lala Binda Pershad Sahab, resident of Rahi, Bayasi Pargana, Jonepur District. The marriage of Babu Sunkta Pershad, second nephew (sister's son) was held in the family of Lala Nawal Kishore Lal Sahab, resident of Setla Chowkiya, and the marriage of the first niece (Sister's daughter) was held in the family of Lala Shiv Amer. Lal Sahab, resident of Hanwada village of Jonepur District was held with Babu Madan Lal, son of Lala Gajraj Singh, son of Lala Shiv Amar Lal Sahab, Lawyer, at Ghazipur. Babu Nandan Lal Sahab is related to the family of Shankar Lal Sahab by way of marriage. The maternal grandfather of the brother Badal Lal Sahab holds ancestral property in English territory. He has also purchased English *Chak.* He has a factory and a godown.

Earlier he was the Attorney *(Mukhtaar)* of Raja Sahab of Jonepur, Azamgarh District in place of my father. Due to ruin of the factory, he has now abandoned the job and keeps himself busy in the godown.

Family Tree of brother Mata Badal Lal Sahab, resident of Sarai Harkho, Jonepur District

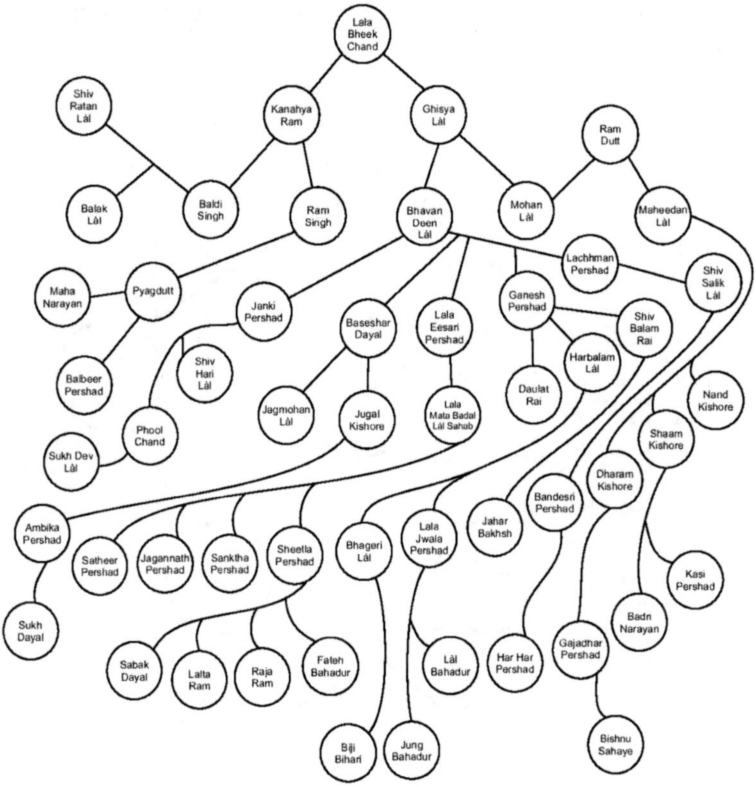

The marriage of the first daughter of my paternal uncle (father's brother) Parash Lal Sahab (late) was held in the family of Lala Debi Dayal Lal Sahab, resident of Meerpur village, Machli Shaher Pargana, Jonepur District with Lala Jokhu Lal Sahab.

The family tree was not received, therefore, whatever I remembered is entered here.

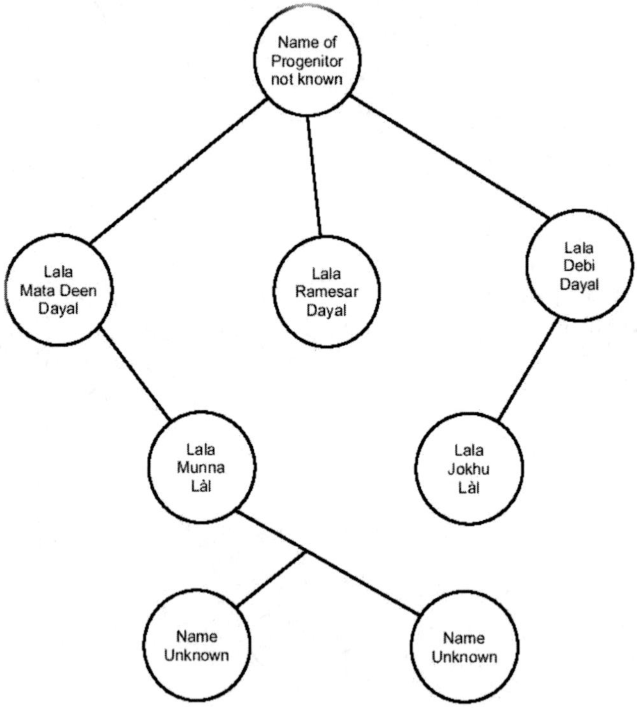

My marriage was held with the daughter of Munshi Maha Narayan Lal Sahab, resident of Saitla Chowkiyan village, Jonepur city. The marriage of the second daughter of Munshi Maha Narayan Lal was held with Munshi Nand Kishore Lal, at Parasurampur village, who was the clerk (writer or *Muharrir*) in Dusali at Lala Mata Dayal Sahab Lawyer, Sarai Barkhoheen village, Jonepur District.

The marriage of third daughter of Munshi Maha Narayan Lal was held in Soweh village of Jonepur District.

His marriage was held in Sondhi village, Jonepur District. In this family also, the office of *Qanoongoyi* continued till Lala Jai Narayan Lal Sahab. At present, Munshi Maha Narayan Lal Sahab is in the Court of Wards of the noble *(Rayees)* Raja of Jonepur. Babu Kalika Pershad is the caretaker in the same office.

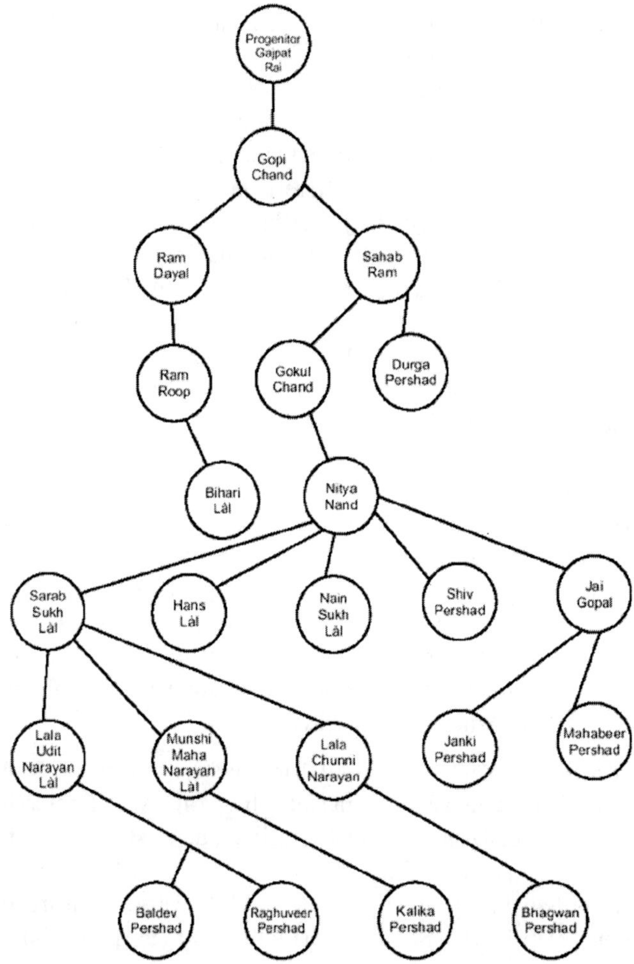

The marriage of my brother Babu Jawahar Lal, General Attorney of Honourable Raja Shiv Pershad Sahab Bahadur, Star of India *(Sitara-e-Hind)* was held with the second daughter of Munshi Manik Chand Sahab, former Security Officer *(Mahafiz)* of Civil Court, Banaras District, resident of Ajgara village, Kathair pargana, Banaras District. Munshi Kishan Chand Sahab, son of Munshi Manik Chand Sahab is at present working as Senior Officer with Maharaja Sahab Bahadur of Kasi Naresh at a place called Konda. The marriage of Krishan Chand Sahab was held with the daughter of Lala Khoob Chand Sahab, resident of Basihi village of Banaras District. The family in which is Lala Arjun Lal. The marriage of the first daughter of Munshi Manik Chand Sahab was held at Talari, Banaras District with Munshi Basheshar Dayal, clerk (writer) in the office of the Registrar who is the nephew (sister's son) of Solanath Sahab *Qanoongo*. In that family there are Lala Tulsi Pershad, Jagta Pershad and Lala Kesari Pershad, Attorney, residents of Talari, Banaras District and Sarju Pershad son of Lala Basheshar Dayal Sahab. The marriage of the daughter of Lala Ganga Pershad, uncle of Munshi Manik Chand Sahab was held with the son of Lala Munna Lal, Lawyer, Mirzapur Court. The marriage of the daughter of Lala Nand Gopal Lal Sahab, brother of Munshiji was held in the family of Lala Mahabeer Pershad Sahab *Qanoongo*, resident of Karakat Town, Jonepur District. The marriage of Babu Bishnu Chand was held with the daughter of Lala Babu Lal Sahab, Attorney Jeromgeer. The marriage of Lala Janki Pershad whose family tree is entered was held in the family of Lala Bindeswari Pershad, Lawyer, Banaras, son of Lala Binayak Pershad Sahab, Attorney. The marriage of the daughter of Babu Krishan Chander Sahab was held with the son of Munshi Durga Pershad alias Durgahi Lal Sahab, Lala Kalika Pershad Sahab, Attorney, resident of Sarai Barkho of the above mentioned district. They are related to each other for a long time but I don't know them. I therefore, enter the family tree of the family of Munshi Sahab leaving them.

The marriage of the son, Babu Palna Pershad was held in the family of Lala Babu Lal Sahab, resident and noble *(Rayees)* of former Sondhi village, Jonepur District presently residing at Wasli Gunj, Mirzapur city with the daughter of Lala Bhagwan Pershad Sahab, son of Lala Babu Lal Sahab. The shivalaya, tank and the garden constructed by their ancestors exist in Sondhi. Baba Kalidas was the progenitor of the family but the family tree of the progenitor was not received. I do not know the relationship of Lala Sahab. I enter the details as far as I know. The second marriage of Lala Bhagwan Pershad Sahab was held with the sister of Lala Bindeshwari Pershad Sahab, resident of Dara Nagar locality, *Siyahee Nawees* (writer or clerk) Tehsil Loth Maharaja Sahab Bahadur of Banaras. Lala Gur Pershad Sahab, resident of Hari Patti is the relative of Lala Sahab mentioned above. Lala Gur Pershad is our cousin (Paternal Uncle's son) and the brother-in-law (wife's Brother) of Lala Gowri Shankar Lal (late).

Family Tree of Lala Babu Lal Sahab Attorney, resident of former Sondhi Village, presently residing at Wasli Gunj locality, Mirzapur District

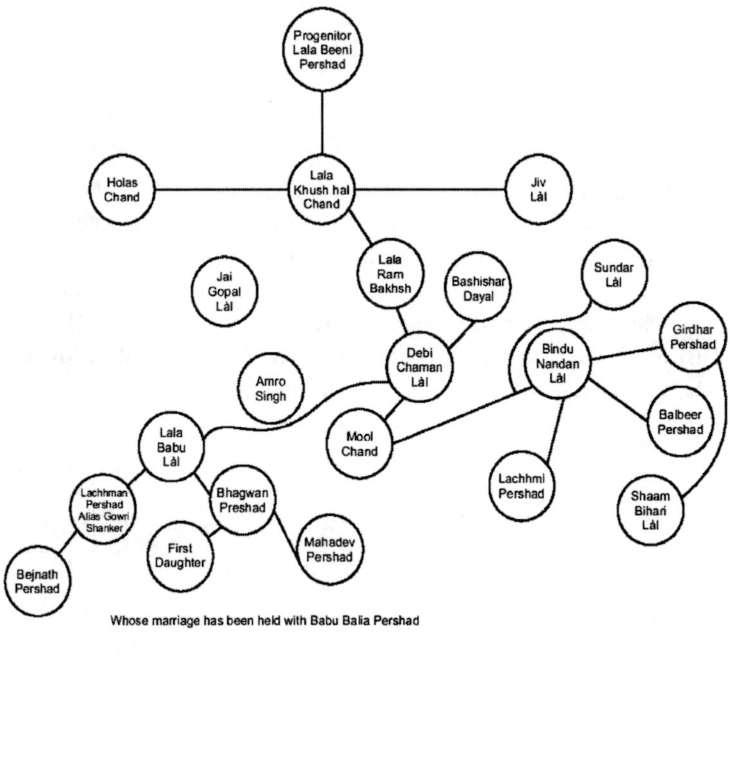

The daughter of our paternal uncle, Lala Salik Ram Sahab (late) got married to Lala Shiv Saran Lal, resident of Tulachak. Despite demand, the family tree was not received. I, therefore, enter as per my memory.

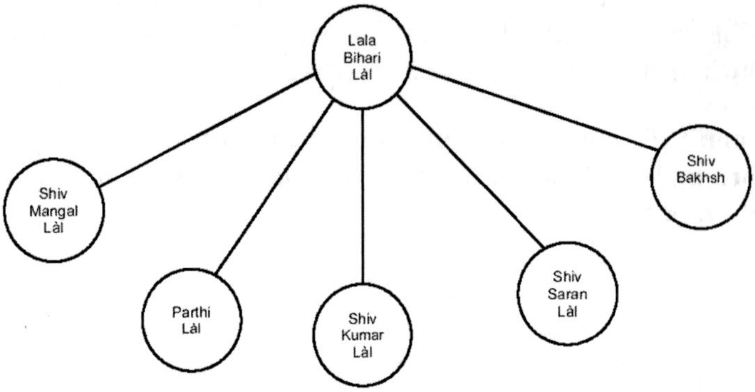

The marriage of the daughter of the compiler of this book was held with Babu Shiv Surat Lal, son of Munshi Dwaraka Pershad Sahab. Munshi Sahab is the resident of Teewar village, Kathair Pargana, Banaras District. He belongs to the same grandfather and the same sect. He is residing at Bhagwati village, and Aasapur village, Banaras District. The details and the family tree have been entered by Munshi Khoob Chand. On reading it, details would be known.

Presuming that entering the Family Tree again would be futile, I enter the details in brief of Munshi Sahab is the relative of Lala Sahab, mentioned above

His marriage hass been held with my daughter

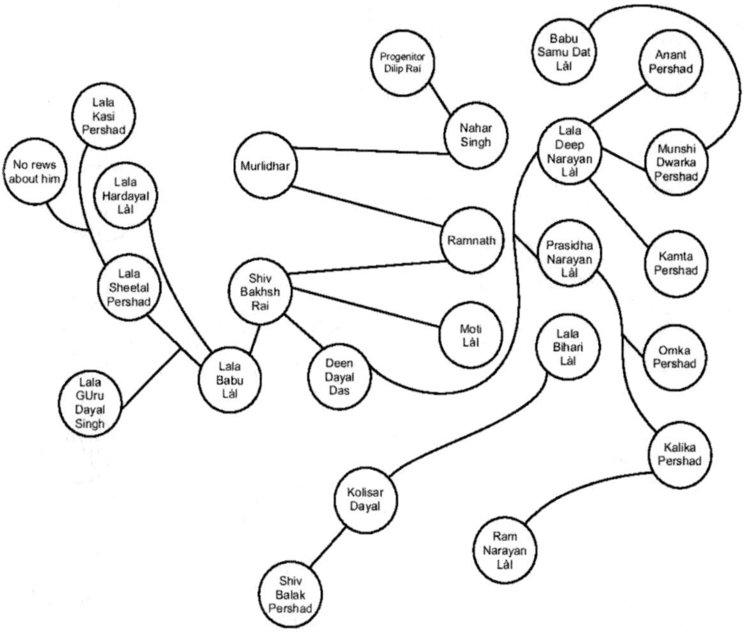

It may be mentioned that Lala Sahab had three daughters. One daughter was married to Lala Khoob Chand, the other to Lala Durga Pershad, resident of Bahnabad and the third one got married to a person whose husband's name is not known.

My nephew (brother's son) Babu Gajadhar Pershad married the daughter of Lala Sheetal Pershad, resident of Pandeypur village of Jonepur District. Lala Sheetal Pershad's marriage was held in Dharam Sarai village adjacent to Setla Chowkiyan in the family of Lala Shiv Ghulam Lal Sahab. Lala Gajadhar Pershad's marriage was held in the family of Lala Jarbandhan Lal Sahab, resident of Daripur, Tehsil, Machli Sheher. The marriage of Lala Raghunandan Pershad, resident of Sipah locality, Jonepur city, was held in the family of Lala Jogi Lal Sahab. Lala Sahab's daughter got married to Shashi Badman at Shah Zafarabad. The marriage of the sister of Lala Sheetal Pershad was held with Munshi Behari Lal Sahab, son of Janaki Pershad, resident of Pariyawan.

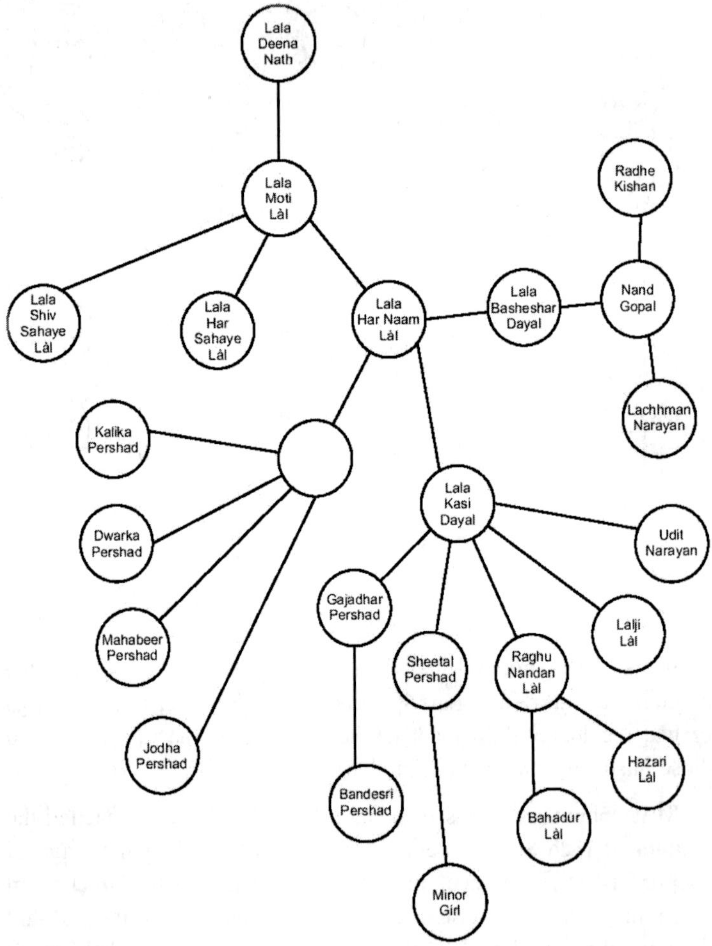

Her marriage has been held with my nephew Gajadhar lal

Munshi Janaki Pershad Sahab, Minister *(Diwan),* Munshi Beeni Lal, Manager (*Karpardaaz*), Munshi Chunni Lal Sahab, nobles of the city of Banaras, residents of Pariyawan, Jonepur District, presently residing at Lahurabeer locality, Banaras city are our relatives from Zafarabad. Munshi Behari Lal Sahab, son of Munshi Sahab mentioned above is my heartfelt sincere friend. Despite demand, he did not give the family tree. I am therefore, constrained to enter the details according to my memory, to some extent, I write the details.

Munshi Janki Pershad's marriage took place in the family of Lala Purushotam Lal, Attorney, resident of Shivpur, Banaras City. Janaki Pershad's first daughter got married to Lala Kanahya Lal Sahab, resident of Sarai Harkho. The second daughter got married to Lala Shankar Lal Sahab, resident at Roti village. Munshi Behari Lal's marriage was held in Pandeypur village, Jonepur District.

Family Tree of Munshi Janki Pershad Shahab, resident of Pariyawan Village, Jonepur District, presently residing at Lahurabeer, Banaras City. Munshi Madhav Lal, President and noble of Banaras City is as follows:

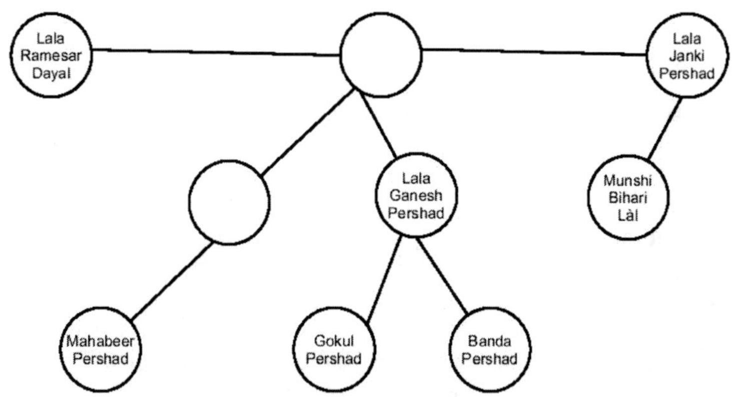

Name of places where our relatives reside. Our family is from Zafarabad. As far as I could remember, I wrote it down:

Asthan Mahkocha	Sondhi	Bhagalpur
Aasapur	Ranipur	Mahriyan
Kotawa	Jasreela	Karakat
Machli Sheher	Kozha	Mohalla Roth
Mohalla Sipah	Mohalla Urdu	Mohalla Banwad
Eisapur	Pandeypur	Parasurampur
Faleechabad	Setla Chowkiyan	Adho Chowkiyan
Porani bazaar	Pan Dareba	Kahrona
Taad Nalla	Husainabad	Miyanpur
Chitra Sari	Macharhatta	Khatera
Bilwa Ghat	Rampur	Pariyon

Relatives of Banaras and other districts as far as I recollected, I wrote them down:

Banaras District	**Other Districts**
Pindra	Ghazipur
Shahpur	Azamgarh
Bhagwatipur	Baharpayay
Nahalapur	Shahabad
Aasapur	Kalletholi
Teevar	Cheetapur
Ajgara	Alsapur
	Mirzapur

There are noted persons in the localities of Banaras City. They are permanent residents. Everyone is related to someone.

Chapter – V

Family tree and a brief description of the members of the community of Srivastav and other brethren like Mathur, Saksena, Asthana etc. belonging to the city of Hyderabad Deccan and Madras (now Chennai).

List of brethren of Srivastav and others who are natives of Hyderabad Deccan. Matrimonial relations of these persons with the members of the community in Hindustan, that is India (meaning North India) are still in vogue.

Lalta Pershad whose title is Raja Lal Pershad Sahab, Landlord *(Jagirdar)*, resident of Shah Ali Banda, former resident of Hundiya, Allahabad District, the family tree of his progenitor.

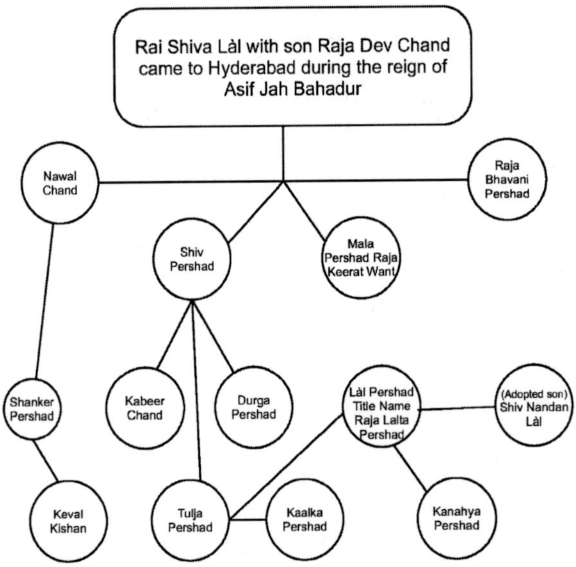

Tulja Pershad Sahab got the temple of Baba Sri Chitragupt constructed adjacent to Aliabad Darwaza. Once a year, Utsav is organised. Members of the community and other persons gather there. Lala Shiv Nandan Lal alias Shiv Pershad Sahab, son of Ajodhya Pershad, resident of Hundiya village, Kewayi Pargana, Allahabad District adopted son of Raja Lal Pershad. His family tree is as under:

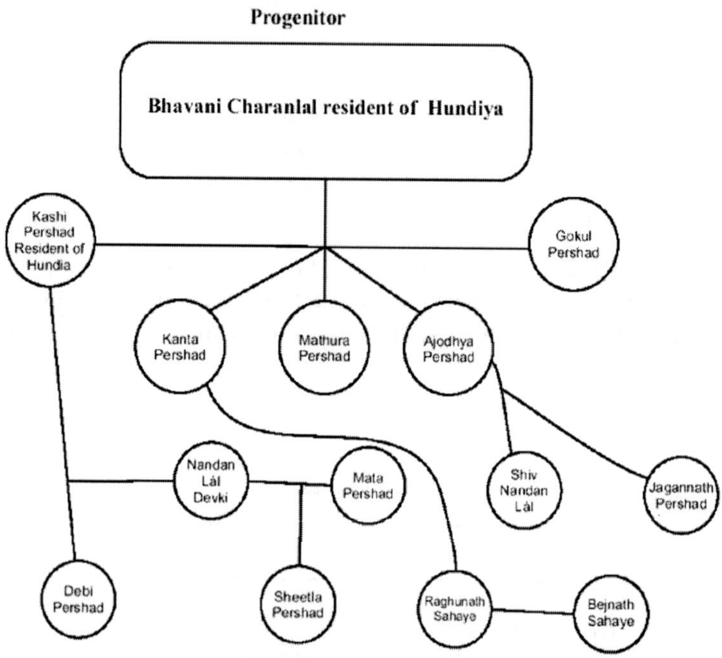

Lala Sohan Lal, resident of Bela Chandu Lal	Lala Bala Pershad, resident of Gowliguda	Lala Heera Lal, brother of Rai Munnu Lal, resident of Dabeerpura.
Lala Bala Pershad and Lala Jwala Pershad, sons of Lala Tara Chand resident of Dabeerpura.	Lala Khem Karan alias Raiji, son of Raja Debi Pershad, resident of Gowlipura.	Rai Kalka, resident of Mahkocha, Jonepur District. Presently residing at Dabeerpura.
Rai Ram Pershad, resident of Dabeerpura		Rai Har Pershad, Peshkar (Clerk) Mahlat (Palaces) Mubarak resident of Dabeerpura.

It may be noted that here, it is necessary to mention the description of Har Pershad with whose recommendation, he came to Hyderabad Deccan and in whose family did he marry? This description is as follows:

Raja Balaram, brother of Raja Ram Pershad had a son, Raja Thakur Pershad. He was the court officer (*Sarishtedar*) of the Palaces. His marriage was held in the family of Jugtama Pershad with the sister of Rai Bala Pershad, who is the cousin (father's brother's son) of Kalika Pershad resident of Mahkocha, Jonepur District. When he died, Raja Sahab's wife had adopted the grand-daughter of Raja Ram Pershad, descendant of Rai Mannu Lal Sahab as her daughter. Her marriage was celebrated with Rai Har Pershad, son of Hanuman Pershad, resident of Achkari of the district mentioned above. This person had come from the above district with the recommendation of Rai Kalika Pershad. Rai Har Pershad had three sons. His eldest son, Chain Rai (Minor) is working as the officer in the Palaces and Rai Har Pershad performs his duties. Prior to this, Rai Munnu Lal had helped this family by working as *Sarishtedar.* He was a very virtuous person. One of his brothers came from India (meaning North India) and stayed with him. He used to take care of his hospitality.

List of brethren Srivastav and other local persons of Hyderabad Deccan and the description of Munshi Lalta Pershad Sahab, Home Secretary of Circar Territory of the Nizam of Hyderabad Deccan, resident of Mahona Town, Maleehabad Tehsil, Lucknow District. His father, Munshi Sahab mentioned above, for a long time, functioned as Inspector in the Department of Settlement. At present, he is working as the Manager (*Sarishtedar*) in Seetapur District. His family has been residing in the said town for the past four hundred years. They are the former natives of Dhara Nagar. He got nearly 200 households inhibited; one of his grandfathers is still living in the said town. The post of *Qanoongoyi* (revenue collection) of this town has been in this family since the time of Munshi Sahab. Lala Desukh Rai is still working as the *Qanoongo* of this town. I, therefore, enter the family tree of Munshi Sahab from my memory.

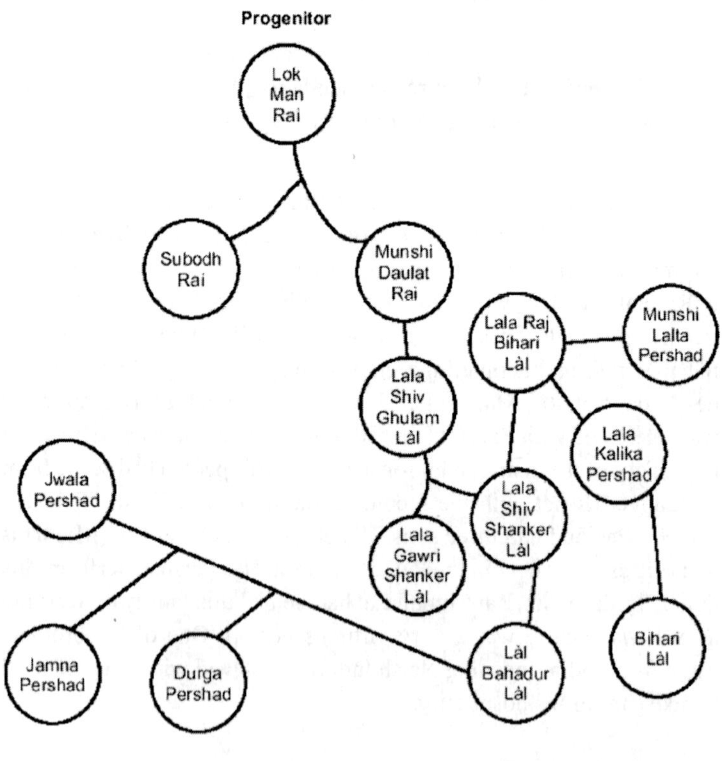

LIST OF SRIVASTAV AND OTHER LOCAL PERSONS

HYDERABAD DECCAN	
Lala Banke Behari Lal Sahab, Lawyer, Grade II, resident of Sondhi Tola, Lucknow.	Rai Binay Bahadur, Lawyer, Grade II, and Kunj Kishore Sahab, residents of Wasli Gunj locality, Mirzapur.
Lala Rameshwar Dayal Sahab, Lawyer, Grade III, son of Lala Lachman Pershad, resident of Gayaji.	Lala Heera Lal Sahab, resident of Saras Gayaji District.
Munshi Shaadi Lal Sahab, Assistant, Dept. of Settlement, resident of Kakoori, Lucknow.	Rai Basheshar Dayal, Revenue Inspector, Dept. of Settlement, resident of Maiswada, Awadh Province.
Lala Bhagwant Lal, son of Gowri Shankar Sahab and Lala Raghuveer Dayal, resident of Fatehpura, Baswan, Nawab Gunj, District, Barabanki, Lucknow.	Munshi Pratap Narayan, Lawyer, Grade II, resident of Allahabad.
Lala Sahab Dayal, Peshkar (clerk), Dept. of Settlement, Baliya, Nawab Gunj, Barabanki District.	Lala Mehtab Rai, Lawyer, Raichur District, resident of Konsa, Rai Bareily District and Lala Ajodhya Pershad, relative of Lala Sahab, resident of Sarsa, Onam District.
Raja Bajrang Bali Sahab, resident of Rai Bareily, employee of Maharaja Shiv Raj Bahadur Dharamwant Bahadur.	Lala Banda Pershad Sahab, Mutasaddi (Secretary) Police Dept. resident of Kanyapur, Onam District.
Rai Dwaraka Pershad Sahab, employee of Raja Girdhari Pershad Sahab Bahadur, resident of Fatehpura, Haswa. Rai Uday Behari Lal Sahab, resident of Kakori, Gulbarga, Talukhdar's Office Section-in-charge.	Rai Sheetal Pershad Sahab, employee of Regular Army, Chief Manager, resident of Maisooria, Nawab Gunj, Barabanki District. ===
Rai Deen Dayal Sahab, resident of Bijaya Gunj Locality, Lucknow. Employee of Nazm-e-Jamiat.	Rai Lalta Pershad Sahab, resident of Mehool, Seetapur, Lucknow District. Accountant in Home Secretary's office.
Rai Ganga Bishan Sahab, resident of Maisoora, Onam District, employee of Dept. of Settlement.	Rai Bijay Bahadur, resident of Hadapa, Onam District, employee of Nawab Sahab.

Rai Bishan Saroop Sahab, resident of Batoha Onam District. Supervisor (Darogha) Bazaar Iqbal Gunj, Territory of Nawab Iqbal uddowla Bahadur.	Rai Suraj Pershad Sahab, resident of Lucknow.
Rai Lalji and Rai Dhanpat Rai and Lakhpat Rai Sahab, employees of Raja Girdhari Pershad Sahab Bahadur, presently arrived at Hussaini Sida, former resident of Kakori, Lucknow District.	Rai Kunwar Bahadur Sahab, Lawyer Grade II.
====	Compiler of this book Khoob Chand and Ganesh Pershad, Beecho Lal, employee of Mr.Thomas Palmer Sahab, Barrister-at-Law, resident of Prahlad Ghat, Banaras District, presently residing at Bazaar Residency, Hyderabad Deccan.

List of genuine Kayasth Srivastav, local and natives of Hyderabad City Deccan

Munshi Mukund Lal Sahab, Assistant, Department of Settlement, resident of Kakori, Lucknow District.	Shri Basheshar Nath Sahab, Tehsildar, Kathair, resident of Lucknow District.
Rai Mohan Lal Sahab	Rai Murari Lal Sahab.
Rai Durga Pershad, resident of Bhopal.	Rai Mehtab Rai, resident of Bhopal.
Rai Chaid Bal Sahab, Rai Kashi Pershad Sahab, Rai G.Gopal Sahab, Rai Raj Bahadur Sahab, residents of Lucknow.	Rai Roshan Lal Sahab, resident of Rai Binda Saran, Faizabad.
Munshi Uday Behari Lal Sahab, Son of Munshi Basheshar Nath Sahab, Tehsildar.	Rai Har Pershad Sahab, Rai Debi Dayal Sahab, residents of Lucknow.
=====	Rai Gaya Pershad.

Brief description of Rai Murlidhar Sahab Talukhdar (Collector) and Rai Bhagwat Pershad Sahab, Assistant, Court of Bidar, Caste: Kayasth Asthana

The progenitor of this family Tiranmal of Lanwan Town, went to Delhi from Hardoyi District during the period of King Faruk Siyar. He stayed there for a few days, went to Swaroon town which is on the bank of River Ganga and stayed there. At the end, he came down to Akbarabad (Agra) and settled there. In his family, Rai Munnu Lal Sahab (late) was a very famous person in Asthana community. Here, the attributes of the late person are mentioned. Despite absence in classes, he gained proficiency in all the subjects of Social Sciences, like Mathematics out of his intelligence. At last, he was appointed Head Master of Roorky College. Many of his students like British Nationals passed higher examinations and distinguished themselves in various services. In addition to this, Rai Sahab wrote a few books on Mathematics. For some time, he functioned as Executive Engineer in the territory of Ganga Canal on a remuneration of Rs 500. Later, Nawab Madarul Mahaam (Prime Minister) of the government heard about his good conduct and efficiency of high calibre and commissioned him and offered him the Head Master's post of Engineering College and Assistant Secretary of the Public Works Department on a remuneration of Rs 1,230. The strange thing is that he developed personal contacts with the nobles and noted persons as a result of which, he became distinguished in the eyes of one and all. Government sanctioned him a pension of Rs 300. It is understood that he was given lands *(Jagir)* also. During his tenure of office, he was a noted person in the entire dominion. During the last days of his life, he settled down in Aurangabad where he was getting a pension of Rs 100 per month. He expired there. During his life time, his sons, Rai Murlidhar Sahab and his nephews (brother's sons), Rai Bhagwat Pershad Sahab, Rai Prabhu Lal Sahab came to this city. Rai Murlidhar Sahab, Collector of Aurangabad, Bhagwat Pershad Sahab, Assistant, office of Bidar and Rai Prabhu Lal Sahab are working as Translator (Political) in Finance Department. His nephew (brother's son) Munshi Anandi Lal also acquired education in Arabic Language. Collector of Agra, Sir William Muir learnt Arabic from him and reinstated him against to the post of Tehsildar and after that, the very next day, this young man expired. All these persons possess good qualities. They take care of their brothers to utmost possible extent.

It may be mentioned that Lala Joti Pershad Sahab is the maternal cousin (mother's brother's son) of these persons. He is working as Translator of an English newspaper in Political Finance Department. He is very polite. The family tree of Rai Murlidhar Sahab, Collector and Rai Bhagwat Pershad, Assistant in the Court of Bidar is entered below.

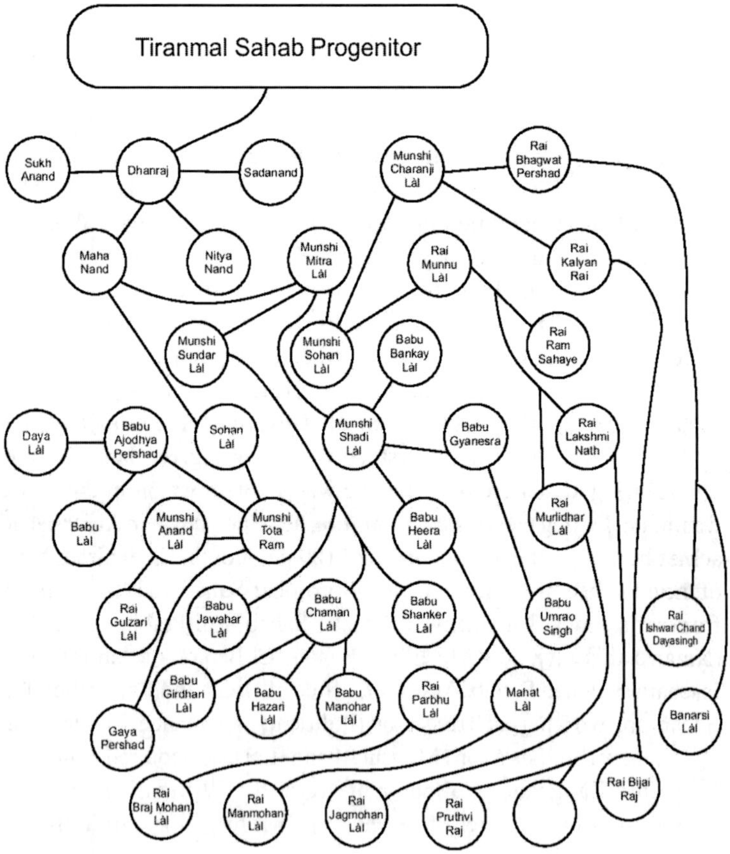

Also See

Sohan Lal was the father of Mannu Lal. Sohan Lal moved from Delhi to Agra and from Moghal to the British Service. He was made in-charge of the Excise Department of Agra City. He played an important role during the Mutiny of 1857.

Mannu Lal was born in the year 1825. He was the Executive Engineer on the Ganges Canal work and a great admirer of the British administration. He rendered valuable service to the British. During the Mutiny of 1857, in recognition of his services, he was granted three villages in Bulundshahar, near Agra.

In the year 1870, Salar Jung-I sought the help of the British Resident to take the services of Mannu Lal and appointed him in Hyderabad.

On his arrival in Hyderabad, he was made Assistant Principal in Hyderabad Engineering School and Assistant Secretary to Government in Irrigation and Public Works Department. This was in the year 1872. Rai Mannu Lal died in the year 1888.

Rai Murlidhar was the son of Mannu Lal. Mannu Lal got good education for his son Rai Murlidhar. He was sent to English medium school. He was also given tuition in Persian, Urdu and English. Rai Murlidhar studied for the Arts examination of the Calcutta University. Later, he joined the service of the Nizam's Government in the Revenue Department as Assistant Tehsildar. He then became the second Tehsildar in the year 1878 and subsequently Tehsildar in 1883.

He proved himself a brilliant and distinguished executive. He was appointed *Subedar* of Aurangabad and Bihar. His remarkable achievement was to raise the status of *Subedarship* or Commissioner of the division. Later, he became Revenue Secretary. On his retirement from revenue service, he was appointed in the *Sarf-i-Khas* Department (Nizam's Private Estate). Subsequently, he rose to the position of In-charge of the Department.

He was awarded the title of "Fateh Nawazwanth Bahadur" in the year 1917. His views on Hindu-Muslim unity were consistently exemplified. He passed away in the year 1929.

He left behind him a widow and two sons, Jagan Mohan Lal and Kanhaiya Lal. Jagan Mohan Lal was born in the year 1877 and Kanhaiya Lal in 1894.

Jagan Mohan Lal had no issues. He followed the footsteps of his father and joined Revenue Department after graduating from Madras University. He had good reputation and great respect among the Hindu and the Muslim communities. He was made Nazim-i-Atiyat (Director of Atiyat in the Revenue Appellate Court).

He passed away in the year 1934.

Kanhaiya Lal had three sons. The eldest son was Kunj Behari Lal. Kanhaiya Lal passed away at an early age in the year 1928.

Kunj Behari Lal was born in the year 1919. He joined the Revenue Department after graduation. He served in various positions, such as, Collector of Districts like Nanded, Medak, Nalgonda and Bidar of the erstwhile Hyderabad State. He was the Chairman of the Service Rules Commission of Government of Andhra Pradesh. He was also the member of Board of Revenue, Government of Andhra Pradesh.

Bravo! These are the happy days. Temperament is full of enthusiasm. The nightingales are singing happily in the garden of wishes and they are narrating the description of the family of Raja Girdhari Pershad alias Bansi Raja Bahadur.

The progenitor of Raja Sahab, Rai Daulat Rai, son of Shitab Rai of Kayasth community sect Saxena with his brother Rai Narsing Bhan, resident of Mandiya, Chabramau came from Delhi City along with Nawab Qamaruddin Khan to Deccan. It is not known to what kind of service he was appointed. For a few days, he stayed at Aurangabad to overcome the tiredness of the journey. He then decided to march towards Hyderabad City. The great grandfather of Raja Girdhari Pershad, Raja Ram son of Rai Daulat Rai was appointed as the Inspector of 36 factories during the reign of Nizam Ali Khan Bahadur. In 1198 A.H. (1783 A.D.) he bought a *Haveli* (Palace) at Hussaini Alam locality alias Chandrikapur and stayed in it. The document of this Palace is still with Raja Sahab. He is still residing in the same *Haveli.* Rai Swami Pershad, son of Rai Raja Ram (late) is staying in the building situated in front of his grandfather. He died in 1234 A.H. (1818 A.D).

Maternal grandfather of Rai Swami Pershad, Rai Jamuna Lal was a *Munshi*. As a writer, he was unparallel. His participation in literary sessions are mentioned. His four letters have been found in the City. His few letters are included in "Deewan-e-Baqi" as his memorials. He helped in the publication of the book entitled "Deewan-e-Baqi" which has been published. Later, he died.

Raja Ram (late) was the grandfather of Rai Narhari Pershad. Rai Narhari Pershad was born in 1225 A.H. (1810 A.D.) and at the age of 11 years, he was awarded the title "Rai" during the reign of Nawab Sikandar Jah Bahadur in 1236 A.H. (1820 A.D.). During his rule, he was made in-charge of Kitchen and Torch House (*Mashal Khana*) of Government of Asafia. During the period of Nawab Nasir-ud-Dowla Bahadur, after the retirement of Raja Bal Mukund in 1263 A.H. (1846 A.D.). He was made in-charge of *Sarf-I-Khas* Army. He managed the army with minimum expenditure and organised it. After the retirement from his service, in 1265 A.H. (1848 A.D.) he was made in-charge of the Jagirs of Nizam Yar Jung and Fakhr-ul-Mulk Bahadur which were seized by the court. In addition to it, he was also assigned the job of *Sarishtedari* of Nazm-e-Jamiat.

Mohammad Ali Shah whose poetic name is "Aashiq" has composed a chronogram as *"Fiqra-e-Jawahir-e-Khidmat"* (1265 A.H.) (1848 A.D.). On the occasion of the birthday of Nawab Afzal-ud-Dowla, he was conferred the title "Rai" and a '*Mansab*' (official position) of Rs 500 per month.

The forefathers of Raja Sahab were always obedient to Nawab Sikandar Jah Bahadur, Nawab Nasir-ud-Dowla and Nawab Afzal-ud-Dowla Bahadur. He served them with honour and dignity in their courts *(Darbar)* and in 1297 A.H. (1879 A.D.) he expired.

Fifteen years before his demise, he relinquished all the official positions and spent rest of his life in the worship of God. He entrusted all the government responsibilities to Raja Girdhari Pershad.

Among his writings is the translation of *"Yog Vashisht"* from Bakha language which is published as "Pothi Narhari Prakash". He spent thousands of rupees in the compilation of this book. After the compilation of this book, he gave *'Shawls'* and *'Dushalas'* to various

Pandits who had helped him in the writing of this book. On the second occasion, he spent Rs 8000 for the publication of this book. He sent 500 copies of this book to the scholars in the entire world as gifts or complimentary copies. In this way, by doing such good deeds, he made a provision for himself in the next world. On the occasion of his visits to Gaya and Kashi, he went personally and stayed there for 20 days. He made an attempt to get the book published. On his behalf, he organised a meeting of the Scholars and *Pandits*. All the *Shastris* and *Pandits* of that place were very much pleased by seeing this book and said that it is unparallel. It is the best selection. The fact is that the father of Raja Sahab was a person of serious temperament. He was the connoisseur of pearls ('*Gowhar Shinaas'* meaning one who knows the value and dignity of the scholars). With utmost delight, scholarship, good behaviour, he elevated the flag of success in this perishing world. He wrote books with eloquence and rhetoric. He compiled *"Pothi Narahari Prakash"* in three volumes and other books. Raja Girdhari Pershad has presented these books to the readers. The maternal grandfather of Raja Sahab's father, Rai Kumari Lal was the *Peshkar* of Nawab Himmat Yaar Khan Mutamadul Mulk Bahadur during the reign of Nasir Jung Shaheed, Ghufran Manzil. The position of *Peshkar* of the fort of Hisaamgarh was given to Rai Kumari Lal (late) which is continuing in the family. After the demise of father, of Raja Sahab himself in 1244 A.H. (1828 A.D.) (1st Rajab) his name and his poetic name *(Takhallus)* remains. He spent his life with prosperity. Sir Salar Jung, Mir Turab Ali Khan Bahadur, recognising his services, appointed him in the office of Revenue as the officer (*Sarishtedar*) and elevated his status. He always used to consider for the progress and development of Raja Sahab.

In addition to this, he entrusted him with the accounts work of the government for two years to Raja Murlimanohar Bahadur, brother of Raja Shiv Raj Dharamwant Bahadur in the Revenue office and appointed Raja Sahab in the court of the Nizam of Hyderabad, Nawab Mir Mahbub Ali Khan, Nizam-ul-Mulk Asaf Jah-VI. By the grace of God, he has been continuing his hereditary service and the service in *Shadi Khana's* Property of the maternal grandfather, Rai Balaram, son of Indarsen. He occupied this position. After the demise of Nawab Mukhtar-ul-Mulk, Sir Salar Jung, his eldest son, Nawab Mir Laiq Ali

Khan Bahadur, Imad-us-Sultanate, in his tenure of office in ministry and also during the function held to celebrate the rule of the king in 1301 A.H. (1883 A.D.) the title "Raja Sahab" was awarded to him and the '*Mansab*' of Rs 1,500 per month was sanctioned to Raja Sahab. He is performing his official duties. May God keep his king alive till the Doomsday to patronize him. (Ameen).

Raja Sahab's book entitled *"Yadgaar-i-Baqi"* is available which can be had from Raja Sahab. In Persian, Raja Sahab's poetic name *(Takhallus)* is "Baqi". In Persian language a book with the title "*Tosha-e-Akhebat*" is available, which contains *Bhajans*. Raja Sahab compiled this book with his ingenuity. After its publication, it will also be made available to readers.

Recently, Raja Sahab with his generosity got renovated the temple of Adakeshav Maharaj situated at the hillock of Chandrayangutta which was in a dilapidated condition. He got a permanent grand building constructed which is worth seeing. It has four doors and a garden of best trees with meadows and flower plants. He also got a *Dharamshala* constructed along with other *Shivalayas* by spending lakhs of rupees. He sanctioned a grant of Rs 6000 per annum to maintain its expenses. The amount would be spent for *Dharamshala* to meet daily expenses of food. He got this property endowed for the benefit of the poor.

Another building, he got constructed was on the bank of River Ganges at Mirzapur, adjacent to the temple of Sri Bindiya Bashini. He also got constructed a Ghat (bathing place on river side) which is known as 'Keshav Ghat'.

The third building was the tank on his land in Hari Nagar. Its water is very clean and it can be compared to the water of the heavenly river Kausar. He spent Rs 15,000 for its construction and named it after his name "Baqi Sagar". In this temporal world, no other monument of Raja Sahab is existing except this tank. According to the Quranic verse "Only Allah would remain and everything else would perish". It is very regrettable that two of his sons aged 25 years and five years respectively died natural death. He paid his gratitude to God and spends most of his time in Keshavgiri temple at Chandrayangutta. May God give long life to his nephews (brother's sons), Sri Pershad and

Parameshwari Pershad, sons of Khoob Chand and save them from evil eyes. These persons always keep themselves engaged in the affairs of their uncle.

At present, the situation of the family is that there are in all, 50 relatives in the city of Hyderabad. There is none from among them who is not related to him closely. Their description is very lengthy.

On the insistence of Nawab Mukhtar-ul-Mulk, Raja Sahab got twenty thousand guns manufactured in his factory and distributed them among the policemen. The experts of the crafts inspected these guns and they liked them. In addition to it, he established many factories. For example, Cracker's factory, Gun Powder Factory, Leather workshop, Stamp paper factory etc. by spending huge amounts of money. In some factories, he also incurred losses and got benefit from others, but he did not have worldly greed and self desires. Keeping all his worldly desires aside, he spends most of his time in solitude in Keshavgiri temple. In the year 1306 A.H. (1888 A.D.) he was blessed with a son, named Swami Raj and in the next year, i.e. 1307 A.H. (1889 A.D.) the second son named Narsing Raj was born. Due to the birth of these two sons, to a great extent, the grief of Raja Sahab has been minimised. The rest of his life, he was faithful to the King and worshipped God. No moment of his is free from the affairs of the world. He believes that "Allah is enough, the rest is greed". The family tree of Raja Sahab is entered below.

Family Tree of Raja Girdhari Pershad Sahab, alias Bansi Raja Bahadur

Family Tree of Raja Girdhari Pershad Sahab, alias Bansi Raja Bahadur

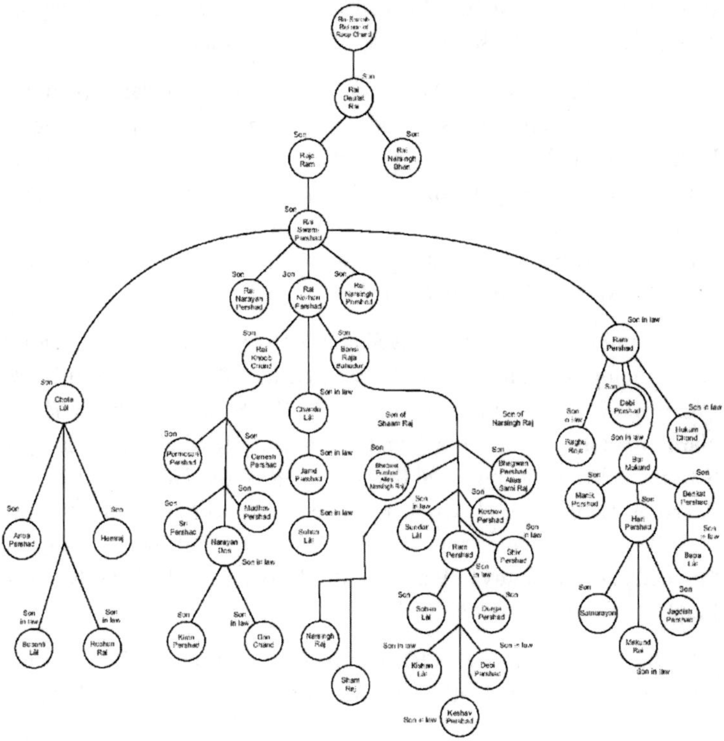

Also See

The ancestors of Bansi Raja came with Asaf Jah-I to Hyderabad. Soon after their arrival, Daulat Rai, the head of the family was appointed Superintendent of the Nizam's Palace and continued in this position till his death. He was made In-charge of 36 departments.

His son, Raja Ram was then given that post by his Highness Nawab Mir Nizam Ali Khan. Raja Ram served in this capacity for almost 40 years until his death. Raja Ram's original name was Ram Pershad, when he was awarded the title of 'Raja', thereafter he was called 'Raja Ram'.

Raja Ram wrote 'Chitragupt Mahatm' in 1227 A.H. (1812 A.D.) which is an outstanding book. On going through this book, it can be said that it has the language of Sur Das and Tulsi Das. Its language is Brajbhasha similar to Sur Das's language and the poetic version is similar to that of Tulsi Das. In all, 53 *Dohas* are written in *'Chitragupt Mahatm'*. He was the scholar of Hindi and Persian languages.

His Highness Nawab Mir Sikandar Jah Bahadur then appointed his son Swami Pershad to succeed him as Superintendent of the Royal Palaces. Swami Pershad was also a scholar in Urdu and Persian besides Hindi. One of his unpublished works *Majmua-e-Asghar"* is available at the Government Oriental Manuscripts Library and Research Centre, Osmania University Campus, Hyderabad. *"Majmua-e-Asghar* contains *Ghazals, Rektha, Rubai and Geet.*

Swami Pershad wrote some Skands of Shri Bhagwat Puran, which are written in Persian / Sanskrit / Brajbhasha. The writers of this *'Sri Bhagwath Puran'* are Rai Hukumat Rai, Rai Swami Pershad and Rai Narhari Pershad. It is in the form of manuscripts, which is available at Swami Pershad was awarded the title of 'Rai' in 1789 by Mir Nizam Ali Khan Asaf Jah-II. He wrote in Persian, Urdu, Hindi and Brajbhasha. He left behind him three sons namely; Rai Narhari Pershad, Rai Narsing Pershad and Rai Narayan Pershad. Rai Narsing Pershad and Narayan Pershad passed away at an early age.

His Highness Nawab Nasir-ud-Daula appointed Rai Narhari Pershad to succeed his father as *Sarishtedar of Sarf-i-Khas*. (Nizam's Private Estate).

Narhari Pershad was a scholar of repute. He wrote in Persian, Sanskrit, Avadhi, Brajbhasha and Hindi languages. He is the author of several books namely: *"Narhari Prakash", "Narhari Gyan Updesh", "Narhari Maal", "Narhari Pershad Virchit Avadhi Bhagwath"*. He wrote some of the skands in *"Sri Bhagwath Puran",* (which is in Persian/Sanskrit and Brajbhasha).

The outstanding contribution of Rai Narhari Pershad is the translation of *'Yog Vashisht'* published under the title *'Narhari Prakash'*. This translation from Sanskrit into Hindi / Bhaka language is considered to be the first translation. This book was widely acclaimed by the learned scholars all over India.

Narhari Pershad was awarded the title of 'Rai' by Nawab Afzal-ud-Dowla Asaf Jah-V in the year 1858 A.D. Narhari Pershad wrote in Hindi, Avadhi and Brajbhasha under the non-de-plume 'Narhari'. An M.Phil. Degree has been conferred on a scholar who worked on the topic *'Narhari Pershad Ki Rachnaon Ka Mulyankan'*. A Gold Medal has been instituted in his memory at Maulana Azad National Urdu University, Hyderabad, India in Hindi language for M.Phil. student. Rai Narhari Pershad passed away in the year 1882 A.D. leaving behind two sons, Girdhari Pershad and Khoobchand.

Girdhari Pershad was born in the year 1828 A.D. Thanks to the zeal of his father, he received sound education in Persian, Arabic, Urdu and Hindi languages. He was a poet of repute and his non-de-plume was 'Baqi'. Baqi was not only a recognised poet but equally known for his writing in prose. He was a prolific writer. He used to compose speeches in Persian for the then Prime Minister Sir Salar Jung-I.

He was bestowed with the title of 'Raja Bahadur' and later 'Mahabub Nawazwant' in the year 1894 A.D. He was also awarded *'Naubat Roshan Chowki'*.

He wrote about 23 books in his favourite language Persian, of which 20 books were in verse and three in prose. In addition to this, he wrote four books in Urdu and four in Hindi. His books were circulated in different parts of India and in Persia i.e. Iran.

'Baqi' was a leading literary figure. He was a renowned poet, as Ben Jonson rightly said 'Poets are rare born than Kings'.

He composed all the genres of verses recognised in Persian poetry, such as, *Ghazals, Qasida, Masnavi, Salam, Hamd, Naath, Qita, Rubai*. His works indicate diversity of thoughts. His outstanding contribution is the composition of the book *'Rubayat-i-Babarkat'*. 'Baqi' composed these *Rubayat* depicting 99 names of *'Allah'*. This was published in 1892 A.D. He also wrote "*Bhagwath Sharif*" in Persian verse in the year 1889 A.D.

'Dard-i-Baqi-o-Durd-i-Saqi' is the outstanding contribution of 'Baqi' to the Urdu literature, since he translated Persian *Rubiyat* of Khaja Mir Dard into Urdu. Mir Dard was a conspicuous *Sufi* Poet. Besides voluminous published works in prose and poetry, 'Baqi' maintained daily diaries in Persian mainly depicting the events in the Royal Palace which are the important sources of reference and are of historical value.

Bansi Raja was not only a literary figure but also a multi-faceted personality, a public figure, intrepid adviser, mediator, a pioneer industrialist, a mentor, an organiser, a philanthropist, a poet and a philosopher.

Bansi Raja was the key figure in the Court of Nizam. He was in-charge of the household affairs in the Nizam's Palace. He made arrangements and organised *Darbars* and festivals in the Palace. He served his sovereign whole heartedly and without any aspiration.

The role of Bansi Raja in the re-organisation of *'Jamiat-i-Mahbub'*, was of great significance to the state. His foresight, sound planning and judgment gave him immense respect.

Bansi Raja played an important role in setting up industries in Hyderabad. He set up many industries but his arms and ammunition factory became a great threat to the British. Bansi Raja was against the British Raj. Unfortunately, his industries were hampered by the British compulsions and their selfish policies, which had a disastrous effect on the growth of the economy of the State.

He was a philanthropist. He constructed many temples in and around Hyderabad, and got repaired and renovated many old temples. He organised *Jatras* and *Urs* of Hussaini Shah and Wali Shah.

Realising the difficulties faced by the public during the rainy and summer seasons, he constructed a pavilion in memory of his father in 1880 A.D. at Hindu Crematorium at Purana Pul, Hyderabad.

Bansi Raja also worked for the welfare of the state and succeeded in developing cordial relations between classes. When there was a dispute between the Arabs and Police, Amir-i-Kabir and Salar Jung-I, he acted as a mediator.

Bansi Raja travelled extensively all over India and some of his travels were along with the Nizam of Hyderabad, Mir Mahbub Ali Khan. He recorded his travels systematically in detail and published them under the title '*Tosha-e Aqibat*'.

It was a red letter day in the life of Bansi Raja when Mir Mahbub Ali Khan Nizam-VI paid a visit to his palace. It so happened, that due to ill health, Bansi Raja could not meet Nizam for a month or so. Mir Mahbub Ali Khan decided to visit him. He wrote a long poem in Persian on the visit of the Nizam. He expressed the joy thus:

'Nazr Dil Dar Dad-O-Dar Pesh Us Aqidat Amada'

'The visit to my palace is a great honour for me. On this occasion, I offered my heart to the king with faith and firm belief'.

Bansi Raja's integrity, loyalty and faithfulness toward Mir Mahbub Ali Khan Nizam-VI is beyond doubt.

After leading a pious and a benevolent life, Bansi Raja closed his eyes forever on 24th July 1896 A.D.

Bansi Raja had a son by name Keshav Pershad, from his first wife, who passed away during his lifetime. Bansi Raja left behind him two sons, four daughters and a widow. Raja Narsing Raj was the eldest son and Mahbub Raj was the younger.

A dissertation was written on Raja Girdhari Preshad in the year 1967 at Osmania University, Hyderabad for M.A. (Urdu).

Recently a Ph.D. Scholar has submitted his thesis at Maulana Azad National Urdu University, Hyderabad on Raja Girdhari Pershad's contribution to Persian poetry.

Raja Narsing Raj was born in the year 1889 A.D. The education of the young Raja was undertaken by the State. After the death of his father, all the titles and honours were bestowed on him. He was bestowed with the title of 'Raja Bahadur' in the year 1905 by Nizam of Hyderabad, Mir Mahbub Ali Khan. He joined the service in Hyderabad State as Superintendent in the RMS (Railway Mail Service) Department and after meritorious service, he retired as Deputy Post Master General. He took keen interest in social activities. He started co-operative societies of Kayasth *Mansabdars* and became its President. He also started a school by name 'Kayasth Pathshala' in the year 1915.

He was a poet of repute. He wrote in Hindi, Urdu and Persian languages. He composed all the principal genres of verses recognised in poetry. He wrote about 100 *Bhajans* in Urdu, which is a great contribution. *Bhajans* in Urdu has a long history but very few poets attempted them. He is the author of several books.

His Ghazals and other verses were compiled by Dr Sheela Raj and published under the title *'Diwan-e-Aali'*. *'Aali'* was the non-de-plume of Raja Narsing Raj in Urdu and 'Narsing' in 'Hindi'.

Maharaja Sir Kishan Pershad was a very close associate of Raja Narsing Raj. He was also a renowned poet of Urdu and Persian languages. After the demise of Maharaja Kishan Pershad, Raja Narsing Raj used to organise *Mushairas* (Poets' Gatherings) in his memory.

The popularity of *Mushairas* organised by Raja Narsing Raj *'Aali'* spread throughout South India. He not only became famous in organising *Mushairas* but also in compiling the history of these unique *Mushairas* in Deccan. Some of those who attended these *Mushairas* are still alive. They not only appreciate the organising capacities of Raja Narsing Raj 'Aali' but also crave for such Mushairas in the present days.

A Ph.D. has recently been awarded to a research scholar for his thesis entitled *'Raja Narsing Raj 'Aali', "Ahwal-o-Adabi Khidmat'* by the University of Hyderabad, India, in 2015.

Raja Narsing Raj Aali passed away in the year 1957 leaving behind three sons, Rai Narhar Raj, Sham Raj and Ram Raj.

A Gold Medal has been instituted in memory of Raja Narsing Raj 'Aali' at Maulana Azad National Urdu University, Hyderabad, India.

As mentioned above, Raja Girdhari Pershad's second son was Mahbub Raj who was born in 1893-A.D. He had his early education in Hyderabad. He was given *Sarishtedarship* of *Sarf-i-Khas* (Nizam's Private Estate) and also that of 'Irregular Troops' at Zaffargarh in Hyderabad. He was a Poet. His Diwan has been compiled and published by Dr Sheela Raj. Mahbub Raj passed away in the year 1931.

Mahbub Raj had three sons and six daughters. The eldest son was Girdhar Raj, second was Janak Raj and the youngest was Vishveshwar Raj. Girdhar Raj was an IAS Officer who held senior posts. He had three sons; Dr Amarkanth Raj, Ashok Raj and Dileep Raj.

As mentioned above, Rai Narhar Raj was the eldest son of Raja Narsing Raj. He was born in the year 1908. He had his early education in Hyderabad and subsequently joined English School in Pune. He also did his Agriculture course from College of Agriculture, Pune and later joined Nizam College. He was fluent in writing Urdu, Hindi and English languages. He was well versed with Persian, which happened to be his optional subject at Intermediate level.

He was an Urdu poet. His Urdu poetry collection entitled *'Gulhai Sadrang'* has been published. Besides Urdu poetry, he wrote and published *Bhajans* in Hindi. He wrote under the non-de-plume 'Saqi' in Urdu and 'Narhari' in Hindi. He passed away in the year 1985.

A Gold Medal has been instituted in his memory at Mahatma Phule Krishi Vidyapeeth at Rahuri Maharashtra, India.

Rai Narhar Raj passed away in the year 1985 and left behind him five sons, viz. Dr Bhaskar Raj, Dr Harihar Raj, Dr Narayan Raj, Dr Janardhan Raj and Surender Raj and two daughters and a widow.

Dr Bhaskar Raj was the eldest son of Rai Narhar Raj. He was born in the year 1934. He had his education in Hyderabad. He was a Veterinary Graduate and did his LL.B. from Osmania University. He served in various capacities in Public Sector and Multi-national Companies.

He wrote five books in Hindi, Urdu and English languages. He has more than 50 publications to his credit on different topics. He passed away in the year 2012.

A Gold Medal has been instituted in his memory for Ph.D. in Hindi at the University of Hyderabad, India.

Dr Sheela Raj was the Daughter-in-law of Rai Narhar Raj. She was a historian of repute. She did her Master's in History and Urdu from Osmania University, Hyderabad and Doctorate from SNDT Women's University, Bombay.

She is the author of nine books out of which four are in English and five in Urdu. She was very well versed in Persian and translated Persian manuscripts into Urdu.

She passed away in the year 2008. H.E.H. The Nizam's Jubilee Pavilion Trust organises Annual Memorial Lecture of Dr Sheela Raj, every year.

Annual Junior Fellowship has been instituted in her memory at Asiatic Society, Mumbai. A Gold medal for Ph.D. in History in memory of Dr Sheela Raj have been instituted at SNDT Women's University, Mumbai and at University of Hyderabad, Hyderabad. A. Ph.D. has been awarded to a research sholar on the topic "Dr Sheela Raj: Life and work" by Osmania University, Hyderabad in the year 2014.

An M.Phil. in Urdu was done in the year 1976 on Raja Girdhari Pershad and his family which includes Raja Narsing Raj, Mahbub Raj and Rai Narhar Raj at Osmania University, Hyderabad.

Thus, one M.A., two M.Phils and three Ph.Ds have been done on the family members of Raja Girdhari Pershad in three subjects and in three different Universities.

It can thus be concluded that the family of Raja Girdhari Pershad alias Bansi Raja is the rarest of the rare example in the literary field whose seven generations were authors and writers in six languages.

Maintaining the family tradition, the family members of Rai Narhar Raj constructed some temples in Keshavagiri i.e. Temple of Dattatreya and Manik Prabhu (2012 A.D.), Temple of Chitraguptji (2013 A.D.) and Hanumanji (2015 A.D.)

Hari Sharan Chabra acknoweldging the services and status of the family of Bansi Raja, in his book 'Hyderabad Personalities' wrote "No other feudal house can compete with Bansi Raja and his forefathers in Hyderabad State in nobility, greatness, simplicity and modesty for which the family is known".

LIST OF THE PRESENT BRETHREN OF SAXENA

Rai Gyanand Chand, younger brother of Rai Sohan Lal (late) Mushrif (Inspector) Toshak Khana (Wardrobe).	Rai Jwala Pershad, son of Sohan Lal. (Madrasi), son-in-law of Heera Lal.	Rai Balaji Sahay, son of Sohan Lal
	Rai Bankat Pershad, brother of Balaji Sahay.	Rai Bala Pershad, son of Sohan Lal.
Rai Shankar Pershad, son of Bankat Pershad (late) nephew (brother's son) of Sohan Lal.	Raja Girdhari Pershad Bahadur	Raja Sri Prasad, nephew (brother's son).
Rai Damodhar Pershad, son of Jwala Pershad.	Rai Manohar Pershad, son of Bankat Pershad.	
Bhagwat Pershad Swami Raja, son of Girdhari Pershad.	Bhagwan Pershad Narsing Raj, son of Raja Girdhari Pershad.	Shyam Raj
Rai Raghuveer Pershad	Rai Ganesh Pershad	Narsing Raj son of Raja Girdhari Pershad Rai Radha Kishen nephew (brother's son) Sajan Lal
Shiv Raj, son of Raja Girdhari Pershad.	Rai Sajan Lal, grandson of Misri Lal (late).	Rai Bhavani Pershad, grandson of Sajan Lal.
Rai Kewal Kishan	Rai Mukund Rai, grandson of Sajan Lal.	Rai Girdhari Pershad, grandson of Shankar Das (late).
Rai Hari Kishan, son of Radha Kishan.	Rai Gopal Kishan	
Rai Bala Pershad son of Keval Kishan.	Rai Jagdamba Pershad, son of Kewal Kishan.	Rai Kanahya Pershad, son of Gopal Rai and son-in-law of Sohan Lal.
Rai Narayan Pershad, son of Kanahya Pershad.	Rai Amba Pershad, grand son of Sohan Lal.	Rai Hari Pershad, nephew (brother's son) of Amba Pershad.
Rai Raghuveer Pershad, Uncle of Walchand.	Rai Walchand, grand son-in-law of Raja Girdhari Pershad's brother.	
Rai Narayan Das, son-in-law of Raja Girdhari Pershad's brother.	Rai Karan Pershad, brother of Raja Girdhari Pershad.	Rai Kishan Lal, grandson of Raja Girdhari Pershad.
Rai Arjun Pershad, brother of Kiran Pershad	Rai Puranchand	
	Rai Chaman Lal, Mansabdar, Political, Finance.	

(*Contd...*)

Rai Tulja Pershad, Nephew (brother's son) of Sri Pershad, Inspector, Wardrobe.	Rai Gur Pershad, son of Tulja Pershad.	Rai Manmohan Lal
Rai Sohan Lal	Rai Sundar, son-in-law of Raja Girdhari Pershad.	
Raja Gyan Chand, son-in-law of Raja Girdhari Pershad.	Rai Kalka Pershad, father-in-law of Rai Gyanchand.	
Rai Lachman Pershad	Rai Baba Lal	
Rai Behari Lal, Father-in-law of nephew (brother's son) of Raja Girdhari Pershad	Rai Girdhari Lal, son of Behari Lal.	
	Rai Sohan Pershad, brother of Debi Pershad.	Rai Debi Pershad, grand son-in-law of Raja Girdhari Pershad Bahadur.
Rai Yadu Rai	Rai Shiv Pershad, younger brother of Rai Himmat Pershad and son-in-law of Raja Girdhari Pershad.	Rai Himmat Pershad
Rai Sohan Lal, Son of Heera Lal and grand son-in-law of sister of Raja Girdhari Pershad.	Rai Mohan Lal, son of Heera Lal.	
Rai Naveen Lal, son of Heera Lal and granny.	Rai Chandu Lal, son-in-law of Rai Narhari Pershad	Rai Bala Pershad Rai Ram Pershad, son of Anandi Pershad.
Rai Ramchander Sahay, nephew (brother's son) of Bal Mukund.	Rai Kanahya Lal, brother of Sohan Lal.	
Rai Rajan Lal, son of Kanchanya Saran.		Rai Bal Mukund
Rai Keshav Pershad, son of Rajan Lal, grandson of Shankar Das.	Rai Keshav Pershad, nephew (Brother's son) of Bal Mukund.	Rai Murlidhar nephew (Brother's son) of Rai Bal Mukund.
Rai Durga Pershad, son-in-law of Rai Bal Kishan, grandson of Rai Tara Chand.	Rai Tota Ram, son of Debi Das.	Rai Ujagar Chand, son of Rai Gulab Chand
		Rai Alam Chand, Secretary, Peshkari.
Rai Anandi Pershad alias Bala Pershad, son of Rai Hari Pershad.	Rai Narhari Pershad, brother of Rai Durga Pershad.	
	Rai Fateh Chand, grandson of Rai Jadu Rai, Accountant, Estate of Kishan Pershad.	
		Rai Ram Pershad, son-in-law of Raja Girdhari Pershad Bahadur.

(*Contd...*)

Rai Debi Charan Das, son of Rai Gur Charan Das.	Rai Khush Hal Rai, brother of Ram Pershad.	Rai Gurcharan Das maternal uncle of Rai Behari Lal, father-in-law of Girdhari Pershad's nephew (Brother's son)
Rai Lalta Pershad, brother of Ram Pershad.		
Rai Sohan Lal, son of Ram Pershad, grandson of Raja Girdhari Pershad Bahadur.	Rai Durga Pershad, grandson of Raja Girdhari Pershad Bahadur and son of Ram Pershad.	

Inspector Deodi (Palace) Asaf Yaar-ul-Mulk Bahadur

Rai Gur Pershad, son of Khush Hal Rai, Assistant of Raja Girdhari Pershad Bahadur.		Rai Nawal Kishore Pershad, son of Khush Hal Rai.
Rai Rajan Lal, brother of Munnu Lal.	Rai Bankat Pershad	Rai Shobha Chand grandson of Raja Girdhari Pershad Bahadur.
Ram Pershad, son-in-law of Raja Girdhari Pershad Bahadur.	Rai Munnu Lal.	Rai Babu Lal.
	Rai Mohan Lal, son of Munna Lal.	Rai Kishan Lal, father-in-law of Ram Pershad's son.
	Rai Shankar Lal, son of Kishan Lal.	
Rai Jwala Pershad, son of Balkishan.	Rai Bishan Lal, son of Rai Kishan Lal.	
Rai Bala Pershad, son of Bal Kishan.	Rai Bal Kishan, Raja Girdhari Pershad's co-brother-in-law (Humzulf)	Rai Gokul Pershad, son-in-law of Shambhoo Pershad, grand son of Sohan Lal (late).
Rai Ram Chander Sahay, son of Bal Kishan.	Rai Basanti Sahay, son of Bal Kishan.	Rai Balaji Sahay, son of Bal Kishan.
Rai Babu Lal, son of Gopal Pershad, nephew of Govind Pershad.	Rai Govind Pershad, brother of Bankat Pershad.	Rai Bankat Pershad, son of Bal Mukund, Officer of the Army.
	Rai Bhoj Roy, son of Rai Gopal Rai, nephew of Govind Pershad.	Rai Ganesh Pershad, Brother of Rai Bhoj Raj.
Rai Roop Lal, son of Rai Bhoj Lal.		Rai Manik Pershad, brother of Bankat Pershad.
Rai Jagdish Pershad, son of Govind Pershad.		Rai Raghunath Pershad, son of Bankat Pershad.
Mukund Raj, grandson of Govind Pershad (late).		Rai Murlidhar Pershad, son of Mata Pershad (late).
Brethren and relatives recently arrived from Bhopal city.		
Rai Braj Kishore, son of Rai Munna Lal.		
Rai Narayan Pershad, nephew (sister's son) of Braj Kishore.		

Brief description of the family of Raja Shiv Raj Dharamwanth Bahadur and Murli Manohar Bahadur

By grace of God, the enthusiasm to write down the brief description of the esteemed family of Maharaja was generated. During these pleasant days, the bud of the heart which was withered for a long time blossomed with the breeze of wish. The nib of the pen which was stained for quite some time, is now ready to run fast on the pages of the paper. So, the compiler of this book organised the brief description of the family of Maharaja which is entered here. There is a strong hope that the esteemed readers would pay their attention toward the meaning and sense of the matter overlooking the terminology, idioms and style of writing.

To describe the details of the family of Maharaja Shiv Raj Dharamwanth Bahadur and Raja Murli Manohar Bahadur is a difficult task. However, to the extent the details of their families are available to show that one of the ancestors of Raja Sahab was Raja Raghunath who was the Prime Minister in Delhi. There is no complete description of the family of Raja Raghunath. A calamity occurred to this family. The house in which they were living suddenly collapsed. No one except a boy named Raja Sagarmal could survive in the calamity. Raja Sahab was nurtured under the patronage of Nawab Asaf Jah-I, and gained proficiency. With the permission of the Emperor of Delhi, he accompanied Nizam-ul-Mulk Asaf Jah-I to Deccan. Due to this reason, in the family seal of Kayasths, the word "Asaf Jahi" is inscribed, which means that this family is called the companion of Asaf Jah and from that time, this family is truly loyal and well wisher of the government.

Initially, Nawab Asaf Jah–I entrusted his private office to Raja Sagarmal. When his honesty, well wishing was proved, then all the official duties were assigned to him.

Once, it so happened that the government wanted to appoint him as Peshkar. Raja Sahab declined it for some reason. Many departments of the government were established for managing the affairs of the state. At that time, government used to function with two departments, especially, from the Revenue office of Maharaja Shiv Raj Dharamwanth Bahadur, the affairs pertaining to revenue, military and titles used to be performed. At that time, the importance of that office was very much regarded. This department was not under any officer, official papers used to get signed by the Prime Minister and the approval of every matter used to be obtained directly from the Nizam.

In recognition of the obedience and well-wishing, of Raja Sagarmal, government awarded him *Jagir, Mansab,* army, a seat with canopy on the elephant *(Ambari)* kettledrum *(Nowbat)* etc. which Maharaja Shiv Raj Bahadur has been enjoying.

Raja Sagarmal had two sons, the elder one was Raja Bhawani Das and the younger son was Raja Durga Das. Raja Bhavani Das assumed the hereditary service on the 17th Rabi-ul-Awal 1198 A.H. at Hemanadi when the Nizam was on tour. Raja Bhavani Das participated in the battle along with Nizam-ul-Mulk Asaf Jah-I. On account of his loyalty and valuable services, he was awarded the title of "Raja Dharamwanth", with the *Mansab* of Rs 4,000 per month, two thousand soldiers, flag and the kettledrum on 27th *Rajab*, 32. He was given jewellery two or three times. Raja Dharamwanth managed the revenue system so well that Nizam-ul-Mulk Asaf Jah-I awarded him a certificate of appreciation with his Royal Seal and again in the year 34, on account of his excellent service, he was granted daily allowance from the office of revenue and military. On 12th Ramzan, 1213 A.H. (16th February 1799 A.D.) he expired.

After the demise of Raja Dharamwanth, his eldest son, Raja Bhavani Das was appointed to the same position. His younger brother, Raja Durga Das continued his service in the office.

On account of his performance, Durga Das was also awarded a *'Mansab'* of Rs 3000 per month with 2000 soldiers, flag, kettledrum and the title "Dayawant". He was given jewellery twice. When Nawab Rukn-ud-Dowla was appointed as Prime Minister, at that time, the Nizam issued the Farman (Royal Order) in favour of his old well-wisher, Raja Dayawant Bahadur that he should superwise the functioning of the Prime Minister and report to Nizam-ul-Mulk from time to time and the Prime Minister was instructed to function with the consensus of Raja Dayawant. So, on a petition submitted by Durga Das, the Prime Minister himself affixed his signature. It shows that all the affairs of the state used to be dealt with the consensus of Maharaja Dayawant. All the letters, orders, *Jagirs, Inams* (rewards) used to be issued after entering them in the Revenue Register. In addition to the above service, Raja Durga Das was appointed as Peshkar of Bakshi-ul-Mulk Bahadur on 2nd Jamadi-us-Sani 1199 A.H. (11th April, 1785 A.D.).

After the demise of Raja Durga Das, his son, Raja Khushal Chand was appointed in the office. On many occasions, he was given jewellery. He performed government service honestly and gained the pleasure of the masters. He expired in 1245 A.H. (1829 A.D.).

After the death of Raja Khushal Chand, his eldest son, Raja Ujagar Chand Rai Bahadur assumed the hereditary service and got *Jagir, Mansab*, flag, kettledrum etc. With his performance, Raja Sahab enhanced the revenue income and curtailed expenses. As a reward of his good service, he was given the hereditary *jagir* and other *jagir* from the government. He was assigned the job of *Qanoongo* in 1126 A.H. (1714 A.D.).

After the demise of Rai Bahadur, there arose a conflict on the issue of hereditary position. Later, the right went to the right person and Raja Inderjeet, son of Rai Bahadur was appointed to the hereditary position. He was awarded the title "Raja Bahadur", *mansab,* kettledrum, flag etc. In addition to this hereditary service, Nawab Sir Salar Jung–I, Prime Minister of the government made him the member of the special council in which the disputes of the nobles and *jagirdars* of the City of Hyderabad used to get decided.

Raja Inderjeet expired on 14th Rabi-ul-Awal 1292 A.H. (19th April 1875 A.D.) and his son, Maharaja Shiv Raj Bahadur was given a white Shawl (*Dushala*) and condolence on 26th Rabi-ul-Awal 1292 A.H. (19th April 1875 A.D.). He was assigned the hereditary service on 17th Rabi-us-Sani 1297 A.H. (28th March 1880 A.D.) along with the title "Raja Bahadur", *Mansab* etc. He was also given jewellery. When Maharaja Shiv Raj Bahadur went to Kolkata from Hyderabad with a deputation to meet Lord Rippon, Viceroy of India, the Hindus of Kolkata welcomed Raja Sahab warmly. On his return, the Kayasths of that place presented the address in the silver casket.

When the meeting of the General Committee was convened during Prime Ministership of Nawab Laiq Ali Khan Bahadur, Salar Jung II to consider the management of the affairs of the *Sultanate*, Raja Sahab was also made a member. Now he has been made a member of late Salar Jung's Estate. Its affairs are decided by two members of the committee in consultation with Raja Sahab. Maharaja Sahab is very intelligent and very experienced. He is well versed with the ancient office which is called '125 years' office. All the old papers pertaining to *Inams, Jagirs* etc. are entered in this office. Maharaja is honoured with the title "Dharamwant".

The family of Shiv Raj Dharamwant is very large. He nourishes almost 300 members of his family. This kind of support to the kins is exemplary throughout India. It is the tradition of the family of Maharaja that the eldest son becomes the owner of the *Samsthan* (Estate). Allowances are determined for the other paternal members of the family. There is no system of inheritance.

Before we end the history of the family, it is essential to mention the description of the younger brother of Maharaja Shiv Raj Bahadur, Raja Murli Manohar Bahadur. Raja Murli Manohar Bahadur acquired education at Madrasa Aliya with Nawab Laiq Ali Khan Bahadur upto matriculation through English medium. After finishing education, Raja Sahab was appointed to teach political affairs to the king. For more than one year, he functioned as the political Secretary to the Prime Minister. He was made member of the committee for reformation of expenditure and the committee for loans. Now, he is functioning as the Chairman of the Palaces of the Nizam, and private tutor of the Nizam. Raja Sahab visited Delhi, Aurangabad, Kolkata, and Otacmund along with the King. He accompanied Nawab Muneerul Mulk to Madras, Otacmund and Bangalore, Nagpur etc. in connection with court cases and Revenue settlements and acquired experience. Raja Sahab is very fond of hunting Tiger and Bear. He has gained expertise in Cricket, Rifle shooting etc. Anyone who meets Raja Sahab praises his kindness and good behaviour. Anyone who comes to meet him is fetched with food. Raja Sahab is very much respected among the European people. The proficiency and kindness Raja Sahab has, is not possessed by any other Hindu officer or noble of the Nizam's Govt. It would be appropriate to say that all these qualities are part of the personality of Raja Sahab only.

Raja Bijay Raj Bahadur is one of the highly respected and courageous persons in this family.

Raja Sahab, meaning Raja Shiv Raj Bahadur Dharamwant's fraternity has 50 households here out of which the following persons are *jagirdars.*

1. Raja Swami Pershad
2. Rai Vithal Narayan
3. Rai Uman Pershad
4. Rai Chandra Karan
5. Rai Suraj Pershad
6. Rai Jalpa Pershad
7. Rai Shadi Lal
8. Rai Thakur Pershad
9. Rai Singoor Pratap
10. Rai Ritika Pershad

Some of these persons were given *Jagirs* from the government Many of them got *Jagirs* from Maharaja Sahab.

In addition to getting *jagir*, Rai Thakur Pershad, was appointed as Peshkar of the Estate of Sir Aasman Jah Bahadur and also the *Sarishtedar* (Army Officer) of the Army of *Diwani.* Swami Pershad is the *Sarishtedar* (Army Officer) of the army of the Arabs of *Diwani.* Rai Vithal Pershad is the *Peshkar* of the estate of Nawab Sir Khursheed Jah Bahadur. Rai Suraj Pratap is the *Sarishtedar* of the 'Mansab'. Lalta Pershad, grandson of Raja Lala Bahadur is working as Collector of Yelgandal. Rai Ghansham Pershad and Rai Jagannath Pershad are the *Sarishtedars* in the estate of Nawab Shamsheer Jung Bahadur. He is also the Secretary of the Army. The remaining persons of the fraternity are getting *'Mansabs'.*

Esteemed readers can visualize that the particle has no relationship with the Sun and *Kooza* (Earthen vessel for water) has no relationship with the river. The writer of this book is like a massless particle and the family of Maharaja is like the Sun. It is, therefore, this pen has no power to indulge into gall or effrontery in this field to write down the description of this family. The bird of this language is not competent to sing a song in the garden of speech but the facts which have been accessed to the writer of this book through research without any exaggeration from the members of the fraternity have been written down since the writer of this book travelled Kolkata, Delhi, Punjab, Lucknow, Rajputana etc. to collect information of many members of the community but I have not come across any person who did not benefit from the beneficence of Maharaja. Many members of the family are in the most auspicious city of Hyderabad whose beneficence is the antidote to the people.

Family Tree of Maharaja Shiv Raj Dharamwant Bahadur and Raja Murli Manohar Bahadur

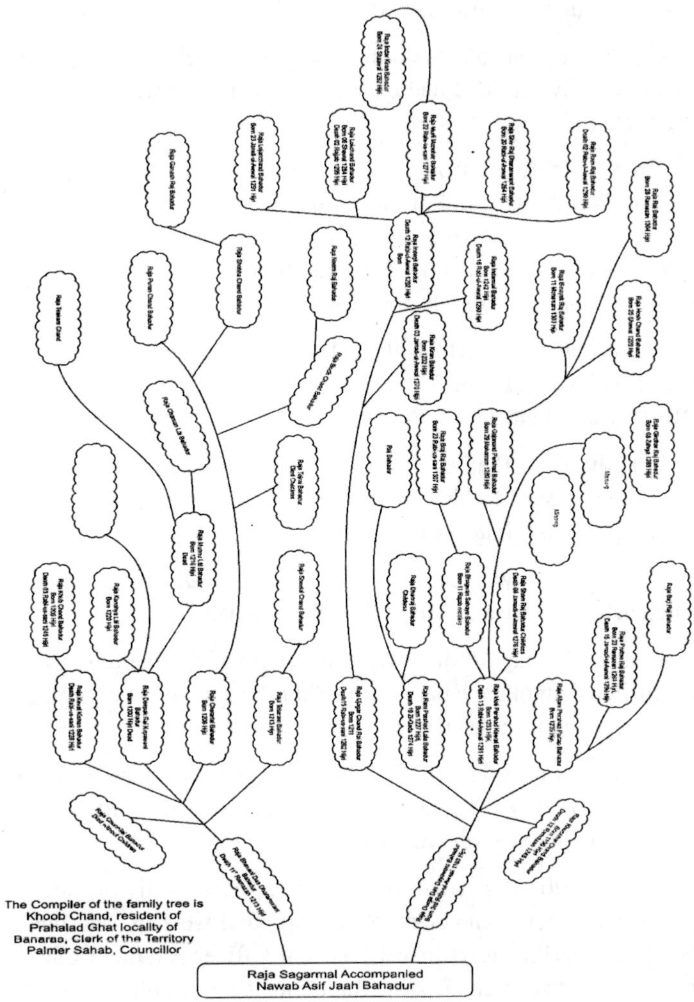

Also See

Raja Shiv Raj was born in 1264 A.H. (1847 AD). He was the man of talent and merits like his ancestors. His father took keen interest in training him in the State affairs. Raja Shiv Raj married in the year 1868.

He was responsible for introducing many reforms in Revenue and Judicial System and had excellent capacity for work and sound judgment.

The title of Raja Bahadur was conferred on him in the year 1290 A.H. (1874 AD). On 7th Rabi-us-Sani 1297 A.H. (18th March 1880), he was given full powers over his ancestral *Jagir* together with *Daftar-i-Shahi* and according to the tradition in vogue, he was granted *'Anan', 'Chanwar', 'Jhalar-Dar-Palki', 'Aftabgiri'.*

In the year 1312 A.H. (1894 AD), he was bestowed with the title 'Raja-i-Rajman' and in 1315 A.H. (1892-A.D.) with the title of "Dharamwant Bahadur".

In addition to the head of *Dafter-i-Maal,* he had the office of *Mansab* and Title under him. He was also the *'Serishtedar'* of *'Mansab', 'Jamiat of Dewani Ilaqa'* and of *'Sarf-i-khas'.*

Raja Shiv Raj worked as *Sadr-e-Dafter-e-Mal*. He was the most trusted officer of Nizam, Mir Mahabub Ali Khan.

On the 10th day of Moharram, Sweet, *Sherbat,* fine food used to be distributed among the poor. Raja Shiv Raj said to have earmarked separate budget from his purse for this purpose.

The family of Raja Shiv Raj Dharmawanth Bahadur was famous as 'Malwala family'. As mentioned above, this family was awarded *Jagirs* by the Nizams of Hyderabad.

It is, therefore, essential to mention *Jagirs* as well. Scattered at many places, they comprised 350 villages and were in four *Tehsils*. They had four Tehsildars, one Divisional Officer and one Collector. They had courts and one District Superintendent of Police. They had many extra powers in their *Jagirs*. They were for all practical purpose, autonomous rulers, although bound by the laws of revenue and political laws of the Nizams.

Raja Shiv Raj Bahadur had hereditary privilege to receive and entertain on behalf of the Nizam Dignitaries from Hyderabad and outside. He was appointed Chairman of the Committee for deciding important cases relating to the Nobles of Hyderabad.

He patronized education. He started several schools in and around Hyderabad. He started School at Enkal one of his *Jagir*. He established another school by name Dharmawanth Anglo-Vernacular School near his palace where English, Sanskrit, Persian and Urdu were taught. The third school he started in Hyderabad City was Dharma Pracharak Pathashala. He realised the importance of elementary education which is essential for the uplift of young children. There are many schools started by him in his Jagirs to impart education to the poor children. He distributed many scholarships to the poor students.

He supported many educational institutions outside Hyderabad, such as, Kayasthha Pathashala of Allahabad, Central Hindu College, Banaras. His financial helps to hospitals, temples and Dargahs are noteworthy. He also financially supported his relatives in Hyderabad.

Raja Shiv Raj had only one son, Raja Shankar Raj. He was born in 1314 A.H. (1896 A.D.) and received higher education under university teachers. He was bestowed with the title 'Raja Bahadur' by the Nizam on the occasion of his Silver Jubilee. He was appointed Superintendent of the *Daftar* but he died suddenly.

Raja Shiv Raj passed away in the year 1343 A.H. (1924 A.D.). He left behind him widow and three sons of his younger brother Raja Murli Manohar "Asaf Nawazwant" (1860-1914).

After the death of Raja Shiv Raj, his estate was administered by the Committee appointed by his Exalted Highness the Nizam-VII.

Raja Murli Manohar was born in the year 1860. He was the younger brother of Raj Shiv Raj. He studied in Madarsa-e-Aliya where he was taught English, Persian, Urdu and Arabic languages. Sir Salar Jung-II also studied along with him.

Later, he served in the Finance Department of Diwani Administration. Under the training programme, he served in Revenue, Judicial and Settlement Departments. He was the first person in the

Malwala Family who took to modern administration. He was the Accountant General and took keen interest in his work.

The Nizam bestowed the title of 'Asaf Nawazwant' on the occasion of *Darbar* organised for Viqar-ul-Umra, the Prime Minister.

He believed in introducing reforms for the uplift of the community. He was genuinely interested in mechanical aspects of modernisation.

In the year 1892 A.D., a Commission was appointed under the Chairmanship of Nawab Viqar-ul-Umra, the then Prime Minister to discuss and abolish all *Abkari* (Excise) rights of the *Jagirdars*. Raja Murli Manohar was appointed the Secretary of the Commission.

His contribution to the Kayasth Sabha and Community is unparallel. He started schools. A Sanskrit School was established for Brahmins as a token of religious service. He also started Mathur Kayasth Club and Kayasth Sadr Sabha; these were affiliated to the northern organisations. Raja Murli Manohar was honoured as the President of All India Kayasth Conference, in 1892.

He passed away in the year 1914. As mentioned above, Raja Murli Manohar had three sons namely, Raja Inder Karan, Raja Dharam Karan and Raja Mahbub Karan.

Raja Inder Karan was the official in the Revenue Department, when a committee was constituted to supervise *Daftar* and *Jagirs*, he was appointed Chairman. He was elected as the Chairman of the All India Kayasth Conference. Raja Inder Karan had one son, Dheeraj Karan.

Raja Dharam Karan, the second son of Raja Murli Manohar held various positions. Later, he became Minister in the Council of Ministers in the Nizam's Government. He passed away in the year 1947.

Raja Dharam Karan had five sons namely; Raja Ram Karan, Raja Sham Karan, Uma Karan, Vijay Karan and Tej Karan.

Raja Mahbub Karan was the youngest son of Raja Murli Manohar. He had early schooling in Hyderabad and later went to Allahabad. He did his Senior Cambridge from Poona.

He was selected to work as Secretary to Prince of Berar, the then heir apparent. The Prince was the Commander-in-Chief of the

Hyderabad Army. He worked with the Prince in honorary capacity from 1940-1951.

In 1942, he was elected as City Father. He was the first President of the Hyderabad Jagirdars' Association. He constantly fought with the government in the matters related to the *Jagir* compensation.

He was fond of sports and *Shikaar* (Hunting). He was also Tennis player, a rider and an excellent shooter. In leisure time he would read history books and biographies of eminent persons. Raja Mahbub Karan had provided good education to all his sons. The eldest son, Maharaj Karan was P.A. to the Chief Minister of Hyderabad. The second son, Iqbal Karan was in Military, the two younger sons were graduates. The third son, Yuvaraj Karan and the fourth, Sartaj Karan were in Bank. The fifth son, Shiv Raj Karan looked after the Estate.

The successor of Raja Inderjit was Raja Shiv Raj Dharmawant Bahadur, the embodiment of the old Hyderabadi culture, virtues of the nobles. They remained in the position of *Dafterdars* for almost 150 years.

Description of Raja Eeshwar Das Sahab Dayawant Bahadur Kayasth Srivastav and other residents of Madras (now Chennai)

Before writing this book, the compiler of this book has written a letter addressed to Raja Sahab requesting him to send the brief description and his family tree. Raja Sahab replied that the book in which the details of his family are entered, brother Rudra Pershad has taken to Lucknow for its publication. A letter has been sent to him to send it early. When he comes back, these details would be sent. When it was delayed another letter addressed to Raja Sahab was written. Its reply was not received. Meanwhile, Rai Kalika Pershad, relative of the said Raja Sahab, resident of Mahkocha, Jonepur District who is also related to the compiler of this book, came down to me. I mentioned about the above letters sent to Raja Sahab. He brought a book from his house which was written by Lala Lakhpat Rai, son of Rai Mata Deen Sahab, native of Bhagwanpur, Chapal Pargana, Allahabad District, presently residing at Daru in the territory/estate Parona Pargana, Meh Tehsil and sent it to me. So, after going through that book and on the basis of verbal information provided by some of the respectable persons of Hyderabad Deccan and Hindustan (meaning North India) the details of genealogy, ancestors of Raja Sahab were known.

It came to be known that the ancestors of Raja Sahab were happy and satisfied. They were living at Chapra village, Ajodhya Talukha. Initially, Rai Daulat Rao, son of Taik Rai came down to Hyderabad Deccan with Nawab Anwaruddin Shaheed. Later, his son, Raja Makhan Lal Bahadur who was appointed to the position of *Munshigiri* (Clerk/ Writer) came to Hyderabad. He served for sometime in Hyderabad and also for a few days at Venkatgiri as per the order of Nawab Sahab mentioned above in the court of Nawab Walla Jah, Noble of Karnataka. He, therefore, settled down in Madras city alias Chenna Patan (now called Chennai). Raja Kundan Lal Indarwant Bahadur got his nephew (brother's son) Raja Eeshwar Das, who was a minor at that time appointed to the position of *serishtedari* during the reign of Nawab Sahab mentioned above and Raja Sahab himself accepted the Vicegerency (*Niyabat*) of Raja Eeshwar Das and used to manage the affairs of the Govt. of Walla Jah. These titles of "Raja Sahab" and *"Munshi"* have been awarded by Wallajahi Govt. These titles were also in vogue in the British Govt. (in India). When the British Govt. usurped the throne and State of Nawab Ghulam Ghouse Khan Bahadur, ruler of Karnataka, after his death, then Raja Eeshwar Das Dayawant Bahadur was occupying Grade I service. He was given full pension. Raja Sahab was a noted and respectable person among the officials of Madras, the British Government and in Kayasth community. He used to be very hospitable to other people also. He used to treat well the beggars, the poor who used to come to him. He always used to arrange fastings for the Sadhus, who used to visit the shrine of Sri Rameshwarnathji. He cherishes the members of Kayasth community of Srivastava with his good conduct.

He is very very kind to other persons of the community and takes care of the widows of Hyderabad Deccan and Hindustan (meaning North India). He nurtures them. There is no one like him at that place belonging to this community. After hearing these attributes of Raja Sahab, the compiler of this book was tempted to meet him. (Everything is indebted to him). The compiler of this book was blessed with an opportunity to meet him, when Raja Sahab himself came to Hyderabad in connection with the marriage of one of his relatives. I met him. I found him to be a person of very pleasant manners and character as I had heard about him before. In fact, he was more than my expectation.

Raja Sahab has few relatives and brethren in Hindustan (meaning North India). They are: Rawat Singh, *Qanoongo,* resident of Moranu, Ram Singh, resident of Kalpi, Dayaram *Qanoongo,* resident of Rai Bareilly, talukha Lucknow, Chada Lal, son of Raj Roop, Dayuwant Rai, son of Fakheeri Lal, *Qanoongo*, Allahabad, Benkat Rai, son of Beerbhan Bikram Das, son of Bhagwan Das, resident of Kada (Manikpur), Bhagwant Lal, son of Gokul Das, *Qanoongo,* resident of Itawa etc.

Family Tree of Raja Eeshar Das Sahab Dayawant Bahadur Resident of Madras (Now Called Chennai)

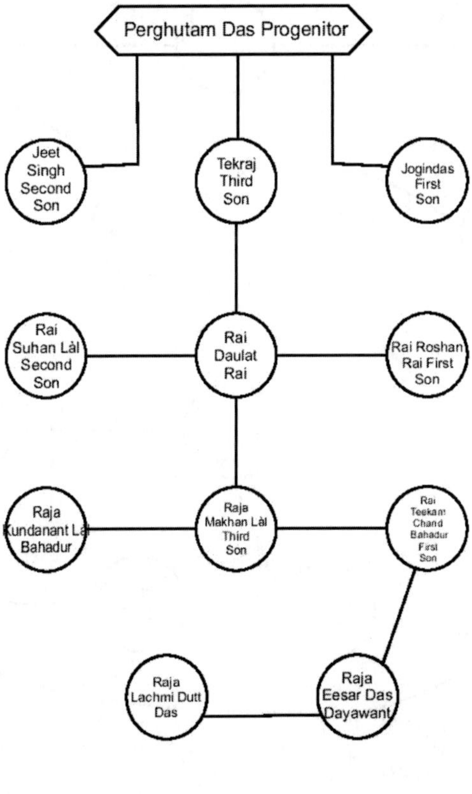

Since Raja Sahab did not have any child, he adopted a boy named Lachmi Das, son of Lala Kalika Das, son of Jagdamba Das (late), resident of Basuri Sarkar Lucknow, Awadh Province. He made him his successor. The marriage of Lachmi Das Dutt was held in the family of Lachman Pershad, son of Gaj Raj Singh who was his old relative and belonged to a higher family of Rawat Singh, *Qanoongo,* resident of Ibrahimabad, Sarkar Lucknow, Awadh Province.

Family Tree of Kalika Das - Resident of Basuri, Lucknow

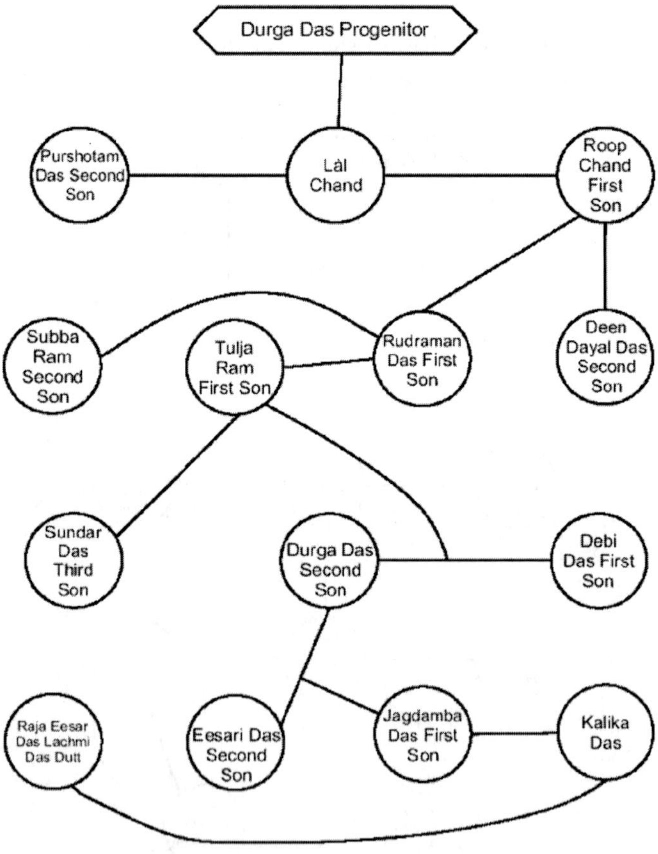

Brief description of Rai Kalika Pershad, son of Lachman Pershad, son of Rai Hast Lal Dakhani, Rai Bala Pershad, son of Jagdamba Pershad residents of Mehkocha, Jonepur District. Raja Eeshar Das Dayawant, resident of Madras (now called Chennai) is the maternal uncle of these persons. Raja Sahab is still residing with Rai Bala Pershad.

Rai Kalika Pershad is the employee of the palaces of the Nizam of Hyderabad Deccan.

Family Tree of Rai Sahaban is this

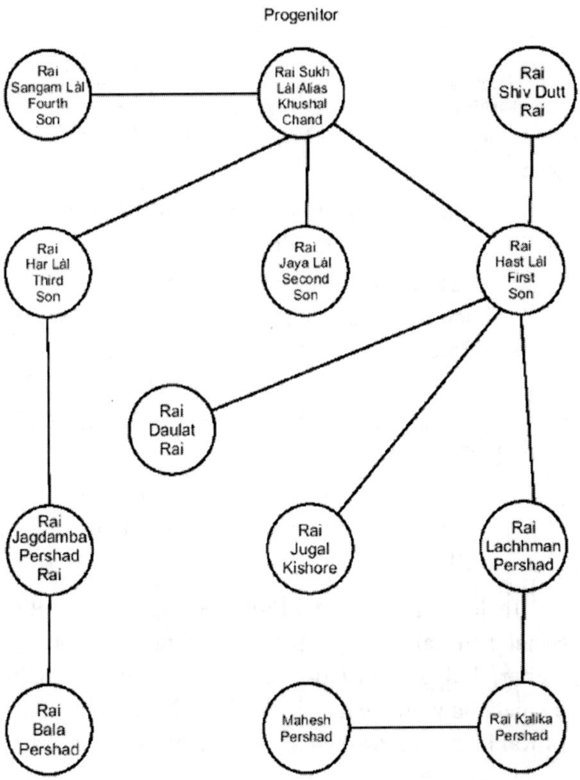

Staying with his family members with Raja Eeshar Das Sahab and Dayawant Bahadur

Description of the relatives of Raja Eeshar Das Dayawant Bahadur is entered below.

Family Tree of Rai Jwala Pershad, Head Clerk (Meer Munshi) of Taluka Raichur, resident of Ganesh Gunj locality of Lucknow

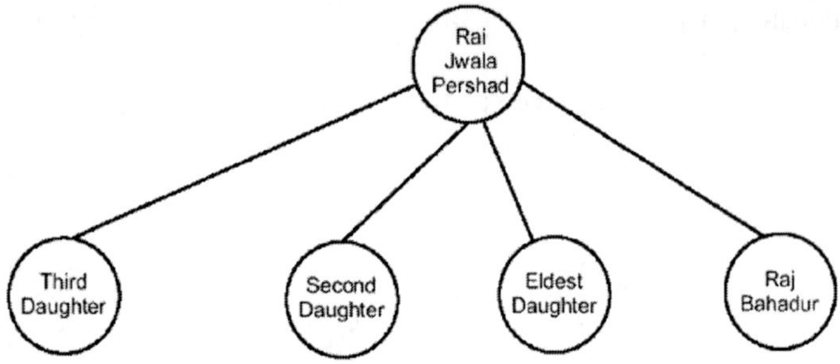

* Third Daughter got married to Behari Lal Sahab, resident of Ganesh Gunj locality, Lucknow.
* Second Daughter got married to Uttam Chand Sahab, eldest son of Rai Lachman Pershad (madrasi) son's father-in-law of Raja Eeshwar Das Dayawant Bahadur.
* Eldest Daughter got married to Moolchand Sahab, resident of Kathra Khuda Yaar Kha, Lucknow, Clerk in the Octroi Office, Lucknow.
* Raj Bahadur married the sister of Dariyao Bahadur, relative of Rai Lalta Pershad Sahab, Accountant in Home Secretary's Office.

In the month of Rajab 1309 A.H. (1891 A.D.), Raja Jwala Pershad Sahab and Rai Raj Bahadur Sahab with ladies, bride and the son, Rai Behari Lal Sahab, Co-Courtiers of Dariyao Bahadur Sahab, in connection with the marriage of Rai Ram Kishan Sahab, younger son of Rai Lachman Pershad Sahab arrived in Hyderabad and participated in the feast etc.

Description of Bhatnagar Sahebaan residents of Hyderabad

Lala Tulja Pershad, grandson of Raja Mannu Lal, Lala Banwari Lal, Lala Kunwar Sen, Lawyer brothers of Bhatnagars are in Hyderabad Deccan. Raja Durga Pershad, Jagirdaar, and Mansabdaar belong to Raja Mannu Lal Sahab's family. Raja Sahab is a very kind person. He has good character. Raja Sahab and the persons mentioned earlier have relations of dining and drinking.

Also See

Bhavani Pershad was one of the notable personalities in the Nizam's period. He was the patron of Bhatnagars and was connected with Military supervising the private affairs of the Nizam.

He constructed a temple at Ram Bagh in the year 1802. This is one of the oldest Hindu Temples built by Kayasths in Hyderabad. The idols were gifted by Raja of Gadwal (a *Samasthan)*. It is said that the then Nizam attended the installation (*Sthapna*) ceremony.

Bhavani Pershad died in the year 1836 and had no children. After his death, all his government positions were inherited by the daughters and sons of Annu Lal and Mannu Lal. The younger son, Mannu Lal was awarded the titles and *jagirs*.

Annu Lal was honoured with different positions. Mannu Lal died in 1847. His successor Annu Lal, continued to hold key position, in the private estate of the Nizam.

There was another high-ranking Bhatnagar family engaged in Military. Majlis Rai was the head of the family. He had five sons. He was awarded *jagirs*. Three elder sons were not married. Chandi Pershad, Ram Pershad and Kishan Pershad were his sons and the names of the remaining two sons are not available.

Tej Rai was the son of Chandi Pershad. Tej Rai had four sons, namely; Tara Chand, Murlidhar, Bansidhar and Ram Pershad. From the available records, it was found that Tara Chand and Murlidhar had no sons. However, Bansidhar had three sons: Ranjit Prakash Lal, Inder Karan and Chandu Lal. Ranjit Prakash Lal was born in 1900 and passed away in 1959. He was a social worker. Inder Karan was born in 1902 and passed away in 1964. He was a law graduate and legal advisor. Chandu Lal was a civil engineer. He was born in 1911 and passed away in 1986. The fourth son of Tej Rai was Ram Pershad.

Bhatnagars were *Mansabdars* as well. Bhavani Pershad and Mannu Lal were granted *Mansabs.*

Subsequently, the other Bhatnagar families came to Hyderabad but their details are not available.

The marriage of the paternal cousin (father's brother's son) of Munshi Ghorset Lal Sahab, Ram Saroop Lal was held in Aasapur village, Banaras District in the family of Lala Debi Dayal Lal Sahab. The relatives of Lala Sahab are Lala Arjun Lal Sahab, resident of Sabhi, Banaras District, Lala Pasupatinath, former cartographer, collectorate of the district mentioned above and the resident of Gorakhpur District, Lala Mata Dayal Lal, alias Munna Lal Sahab resident of Kabeer Chowraha, Banaras City, Lala Binayak Pershad, Lawyer, Lala Bhagwan Pershad, Lala Hanumant Pershad Attorney, belong to the same forefather and the same sect of Lala Sahab. The relatives of Lala Sahab are in Ajgar village, Holi Panday locality, Banaras District and in the family of Deewan Bandhu Lal Sahab, resident of Poorani Bazar locality, Jonepur District.

Family Tree of Lala Debi Dayal Sahab

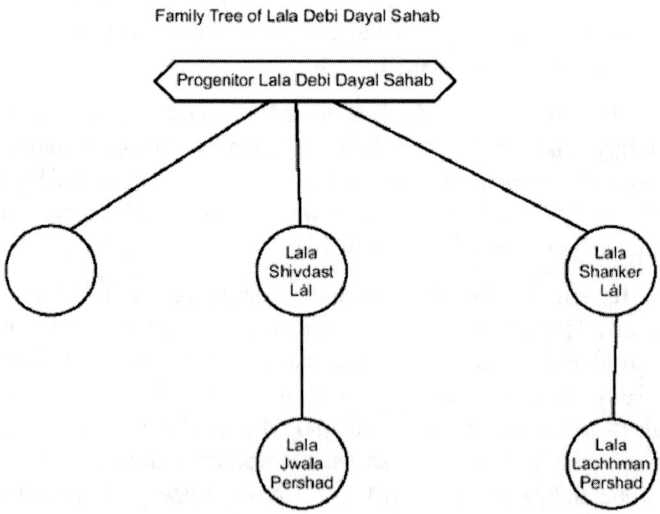

Sri Bish Nathji and Sri Chitraguptji Maharaj's book "Kayasth Kul Nirnay" (Determination of Kayasth sects) dated 31st December 1892 equivalent to Pousya Sadia 13, 1949, 11th Jamadi-ul-Aakhir 1310 A.H. 27th Behman 1302 F at Residency Bazaar, Hyderabad Deccan got printed nicely at Aaftab-e-Deccan Press.

Appendix

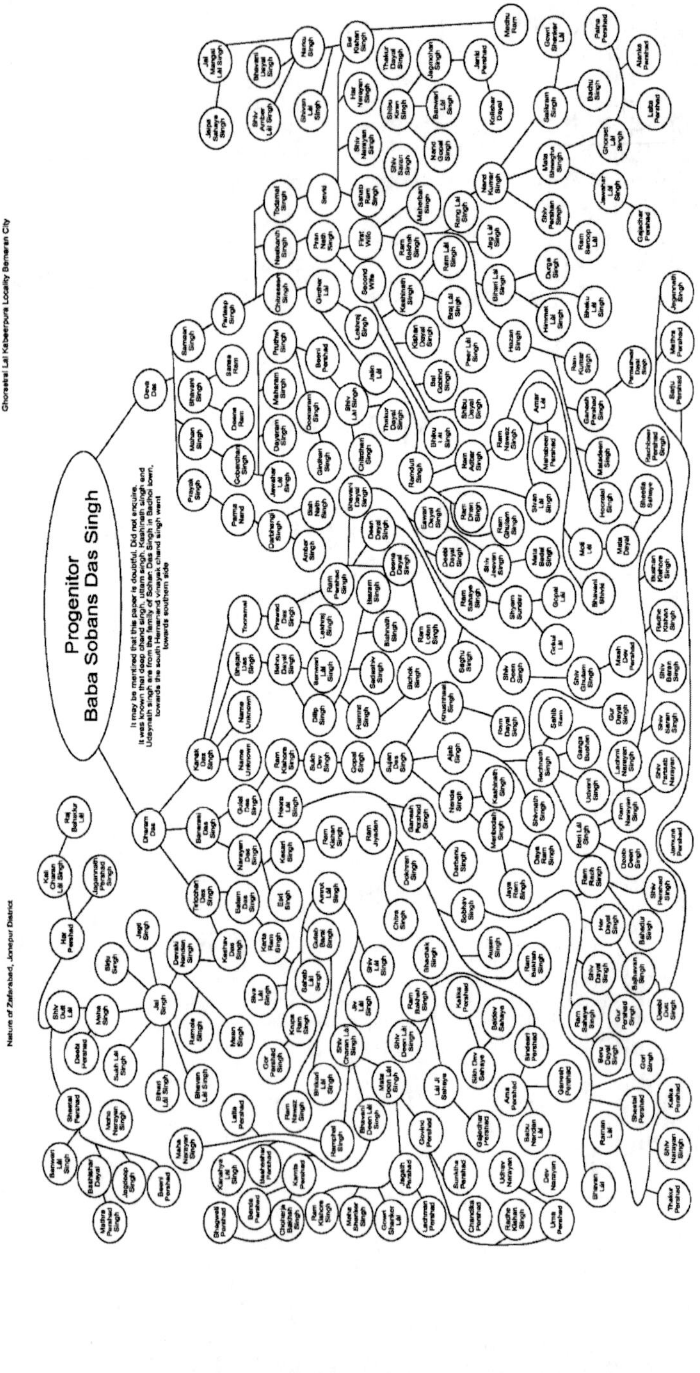
Nature of Zafarabad, Jonepur District
Ghorastral Lal Kabeerpura Locality Banaran City
Progenitor
Baba Sobans Das Singh
It may be mentired that this paper is doubtful. Did not enquire.
It was known that deep chand singh, uttam singh, Kashinath singh and
Udaynath singh are from the family of Sohan Das Singh in Badhoi town,
towards the south Hemanand vinayak chand singh went
towards southern side

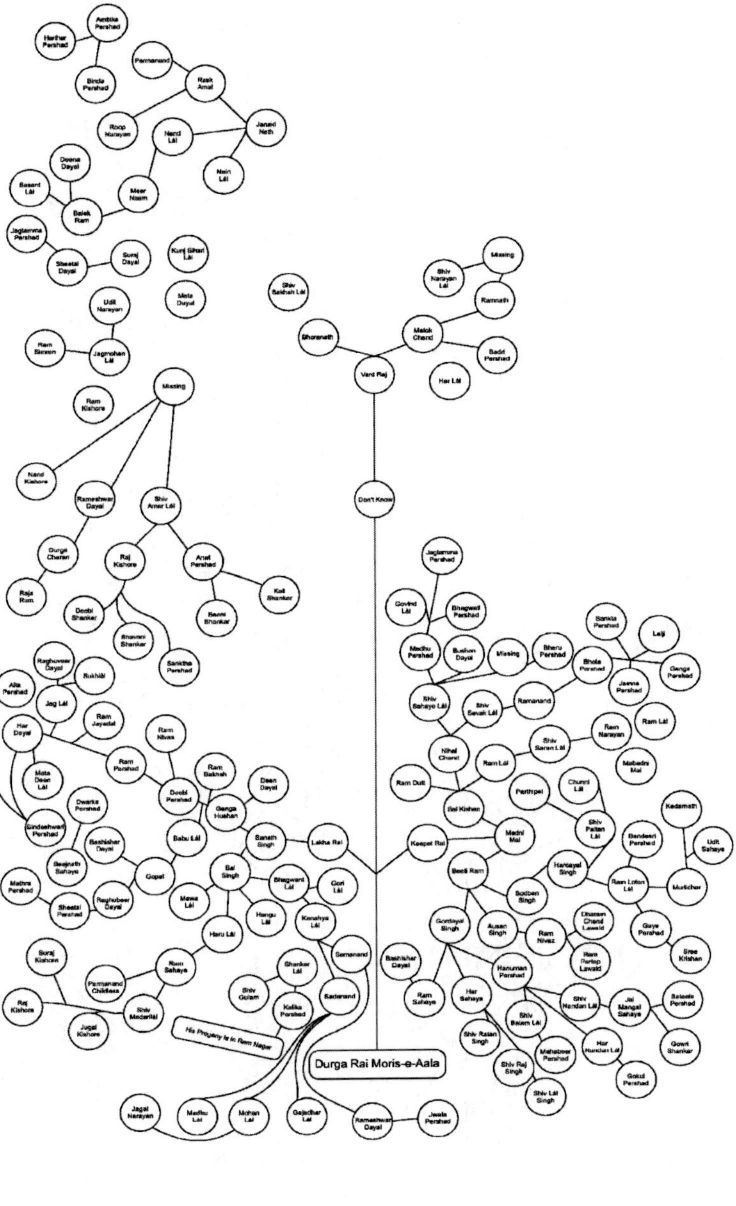
His Progeny is in Ram Nagar
Durga Rai Moris-e-Aala

Family tree of Munshi Manik Chand Sahab Farmer Curator, Office of the Civil Court. Native of Afgara village Jorepur District

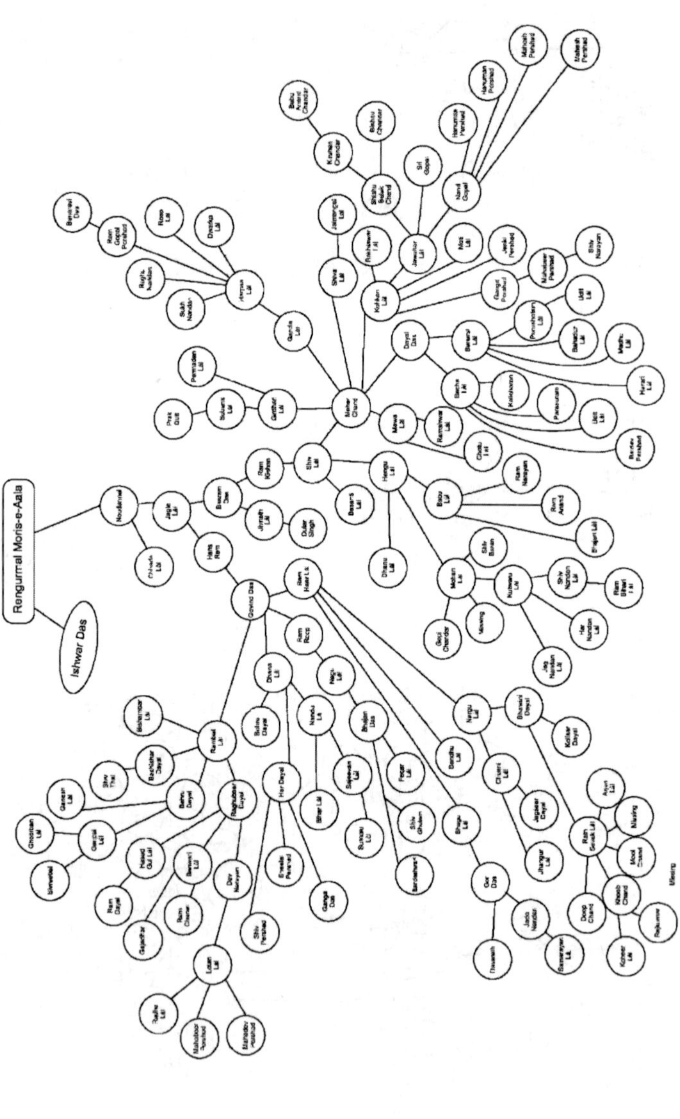

PART-II

Selected Renowned Kayasths of 20th Century

By

Dr. Narayan Raj

Introduction

Kayasthas are considered to be literate scribe caste. They played an important role right from the early centuries. They contributed to the development of culture with their natural talents and outstanding capabilities.

'Kayasth Kul Nirnay' gives the complete details of the origin of Kayasths, their caste and history in different periods. Their contribution and the caste disputes have been highlighted.

'Kayasth Kul Nirnay' has not only covered the genealogy of some of the Kayasth families but also highlighted their contribution in different fields till the end of 19th century. This has already been dealt with in Part-1 of this book.

The Part-II of the book covers the contributions of select renowned Kayasths in the 20th century.

Kayasth community is spread throughout India and it is known by its last name and *'Als'*. It is a practice that the marriage within the same *'Al'* was not permitted but this was not operated restrictively, these days, families within the same *'Al'* have married with one another. The *'Als'* were stated to be purely nominal and no longer relevant in arranging marriages and it has become acceptable.

In the North India, there are different *'Als'*, whereas in the East the 'Als' are different. The *'Als'* are used by all Kayasths, such as, Mathurs, Saxenas, Bhatnagars, Nigams, Shrivastavs and Asthanas etc.

Kayasths played a prominent role in the pre-independent era. As mentioned earlier, they were holding important positions in the Princely

States. Some of them were *Diwans* or the Prime Minister of State. They were into Administration, Finance and Law etc. of the State and their contribution is noteworthy. Some of them were at the heart of their rulers due to their competence, honesty and ability.

Kayasths produced some renowned literary personalities in the Pre-Independent era. These literary personalities whole heartedly participated in the Independence Movement and several of them had to go to jail during the freedom struggle for their motherland. Netaji Subhash Chandra Bose took active part in the independence movement.

The names of spiritual Kayasth leaders like Swami Vivekananda and Sri Aurobindo Ghosh are written in golden letters in the history of India. The name of Maharishi Mahesh Yogi is noteworthy, whose contribution was immense.

Throughout, Kayasths were peace-loving class and believed in non-violence. Their sincerity, dedication toward the work and honesty is beyond doubt.

In the independent India, Kayasths also played important roles in Politics, Administration, Finance, Law and Justice, Science and other disciplines.

The first President of India was Dr. Rajendra Prasad. The second Prime Minster of India was Lal Bahadur Shastri, both were Kayasths. Justice Jagdish Sharan Verma was the Chief Justice of India and was on the commissions appointed by the Government of India.

Kayasths were the Ministers in Central Cabinet during the second half of 20th Century. Sri Jyoti Basu, a Kayasth, was the Chief Minister of West Bengal. So also, Sri Shiv Charan Mathur was the Chief Minister of Rajasthan. Biju Patnaik, another Kayasth was the Chief Minister of Orissa.

Among the Kayasth politicians, the names of Lok Nayak Jayprakash Narayan, Yashwant Sinha (who was the Finance Minister of Government of India), Bala Sahab Thackray need special mention. There were many other Kayasths who played a prominent role in Indian Politics during the 20th century.

The contribution of Dr. Shanti Swaroop Bhatnagar in the fields of Science and Technology is unparallel. He is considered the father of

'National Laboratories in India'. Another Kayasth Scientist whose name needs special mention is Dr. Prabhu Lal Bhatnagar. These are many others who contributed to the nation in the scientific field.

Among the Kayasth historians the name of Sri Jadunath Sarkar needs special mention. He occupied a prominent position among the historians. The others are Banarsi Lal Saxena etc.

It is an accepted fact that Kayasths contributed to the development of many languages, such as, Hindi, Sanskrit, Persian, Urdu and many others. Prominent among them are Munshi Prem Chand born as Dhanpat Rai Srivastav, Ram Babu Saxena, Maha Devi Verma, Harivansh Rai Bachchan, Dr. Vrindavan Lal Verma, Firaq Gorakhpuri etc. Firaq Gorakhpuri was a Professor of English but wrote poetry in Urdu.

It is a fact that right from the Mughal period the contribution of Kayasths to Persian and Urdu literature is unparallel. "Raja Girdhari Pershad", 'Baqi' translated Rubaiyat of Khaja Mir Dard from Persian into Urdu. "Raja Makhan Lal" 'Saqi' translated the 'Kuliyat-i-Omar Khayyam' from Persian into Urdu.

Dr. Rajendra Prasad was the leading Advocate of his time and even went to England to assist his senior in a case, in Privy Council. The leading Kayasth Lawyer of the Supreme Court of India is Ravi Shankar Prasad. There are many other lawyers who are working as Legal Advisors in various capacities.

Among the bureaucrats, the name of Sri Sarat Kumar Ghosh, ICS, first Indian Chief Justice of Rajasthan tops the list. There are many other Kayasths who served in various capacities as bureaucrats.

The Kayasths were also appointed on the Commissions and Enquiry Committees set up by Government of India and various State Governments.

Kayasths are also in Film Industry, Fine Arts and Culture, Advertising, Sports and other disciplines.

It can, therefore, be concluded that Kayasths played very important role in various disciplines during the 20th century.

Two Kayasths, Dr. Rajendra Prasad and Lal Bahadur Shastri were awarded **"Bharat Ratna"** the highest civilian award by Government of India.

Dr. Shanti Swaroop Bhatnagar was awarded **'Knight Bachelor'** (1945) and **'Padma Bhushan'** (1954), Maha Devi Verma was awarded **'Gyanpeeth'** award in 1982, **'Padma Bhushan'** in 1956 and **'Padma Vibhushan'** in 1985.

Many other Kayasths are the recipients of different awards and distinctions for their meritorious services. All of them could not be covered.

Only very few renowned Kayasths have been covered in Part-II of this book, not much work has been done on the contribution of Kayasth Community of 20th century. It is the need of the hour to thoroughly research on the Kayasth community and present their Socio, Economic, Administrative and cultural contributions to society and readers. The research work should also be carried out on the genealogy of each family to the extent possible.

Hopefully, some writers will take up the task and carry out the work in near future, which will enable the present generation to know the sacrifices and contributions of the Kayasth community to the Nation.

Dr Rajendra Prasad

Dr. Rajendra Prasad was born on December 3, 1884 in Zeradai in Siwan District of Bihar. His grandfather was Misrilal who died at the young age. He left a child Mahadev Sahai, his father, in the care of Chaudhur Lal, his elder brother. Chaudhur Lal had a son, Jagdev Sahai. He brought up Mahadev Sahai too as his son. Chaudhur Lal had a great reputation in Hathna Estate. He rose to the position of *Deewan* and worked in this capacity for 25 years, when Maharaj Chhatradhari Sahai was occupying the *Gaddi* who had great regard for Chaudhur Lal. Chaudhur Lal made arrangements for the education of his son, Jagdev Sahai and also Mahadev Sahai.

Dr. Rajendra Prasad's father Mahadev Sahai was a scholar of Sanskrit and Persian. His mother, Kamleshwari Devi was a religious woman. A Muslim scholar was appointed to teach Hindi, Persian and Arthmetic to Rajendra Prasad. After completing elementary education, he was sent to Chappra District School. He married Rajwanshi at the age of 13 when he was studying in 5th standard. He graduated in the 1st division in March 1905. He did his M.A. in Economics in 1907 from Calcutta University. Once impressed with his intellect, an examiner wrote in his answer sheet 'Examinee is better than Examiner'. Later, he did Law and Doctorate (Ph.D) from Allahabad University in 1937. He was Professor of English and Economics. He practiced Law in Bihar High Court. Later, in 1920 he left his legal practice, and joined politics and devoted his full time in Independence Movement.

He also knew English. He used to lecture in Bhojpuri and Bengali languages. He was deeply involved in social work. He was associated with many social organizations like Bihar Seva Samithi. He was President of Bihar Students' Union and Bihar Lawyers' Association.

He was closely associated with Bihar Vidyapaeeth and Sadaquat Ashram.

He was one of the Directors of the newspaper "Search Light". Later, this paper became a full-fledged organ of Congress Party.

He was a strong believer in Hindu-Muslim Unity and non-violence. He was of the view that violence breeds violence. He believed that we should have faith in truth and justice and adopt the creed of non-violence forever. The Hindu-Muslim question can be solved only by non-violence. If violence is adopted, it will lead to ultimate destruction of both the communities.

He first met Gandhiji in the year 1916 and thereafter they were closely associated for decades. On the eve of Gaya Congress, the Hindus thought of holding Hindu Sabha. Pandit Madan Mohan Malviya was persuaded to accept Presidentship. Dr. Rajendra Prasad was made the Chairman of the reception committee.

He was elected Chairman of Patna Municipal Committee in 1927. During this period many administrative and social reforms were introduced and implemented.

He was elected President of Janupur Session of Kayasth Conference. Two resolutions were adopted by the Conference. First to ban acceptance of *Tilak* and Dowry and no one should participate in the marriages where this condition is not honoured. The second called for marital connection among the different sub-sectors of Kayasth Community. The first is not honoured till date. The second, however, has become common among the Kayasths.

The scholars of repute visited Bihar Vidyapeeth. Later, their association became the basis for founding Bharatiya Itihas Parishad. Later, Dr.Rajendra Prasad's attention was diverted to *Khadi* work.

Dr. Rajendra Prasad visited England to assist his senior Counsel in connection with the case of Maharaja of Dumraon who had filed an appeal in Privy Council of U.K. in Burma case.

He took active part in opposing Simon Commission's visit and participated in Salt Satyagraha. Gandhiji was convinced that *Satyagraha* was the best thing to undertake and he was sure that it would galvanize the whole country.

He attended Allahabad Unity Conference, which was attended by prominent Hindu, Muslim, Sikh and Christian leaders. Maharaja of Alwar went to Allahabad and addressed the conference.

After the death of his elder brother, Dr. Rajendra Prasad passed through the darkest days of his life. Debts heavily over burdened his shoulders. He was thankful to Jamnalal for his generosity and help, so also, to Ghanshyam Das Birla. He was appreciative of the courage, devotion and affection of his nephew and son during those difficult days.

In 1932, he was elected President of Bombay Session of Congress. A grand reception was accorded to him at Bombay.

He was invited to preside over Hindi Sahitya Sammelan at Nagpur. He was of the view that foreign words whether Arabic, Persian or English origin should be freely absorbed in Hindi. He was also of the opinion that Hindi must borrow from other Indian languages and dialects. A Rashtra Bhasha Parichay Samithi was to undertake the propagation of Hindi in Non-Hindi states.

Gandhiji founded another organization called Rashtra Bhasha Parishad for which he sought the cooperation of Hindi and Urdu scholars. The work was entrusted to Mr. K.M. Munshi who tried to take the help of Munshi Premchand and Moulvi Abdul Haq. At the very first meeting, Abdul Haq could not see eye-to-eye to K.M. Munshi. However, Premchand brought out a journal called "Hans" under the auspices of the Parishad. Unfortunately, Premchand passed away and afterwards the Parishad was dissolved.

Dr. Rajendra Prasad was the member of Gandhi Sevak Sangh. The main aim of the Sangh was to provide opportunities to villagers to meet Gandhiji.

Dr. Rajendra Prasad went to jail several times in connection with Freedom Movement. He was also put in Bankipur Jail. He was imprisoned during the 'Salt Satyagraha' in 1931 and 'Quit India Movement' in 1942.

Dr. Rajendra Prasad wrote a book in jail, its manuscript was voluminous. He was opposed to the formation of Pakistan and was of the view that Pakistan was not the practical proposition. In January

1946, the book entitled *"India Divided"* came out. All the copies were sold-out within a month. The second edition came out after two months.

He wrote major portion of his reminiscences in jail. The reminiscence or the autobiography was in Hindi. A Federation of Goshala was formed with a permanent registered office at Sadaqat Ashram, when Dr. Rajendra Prasad started a model Goshala.

Dr. Rajendra Prasad was included on the interim Government Cabinet though, he was reluctant. Interim Govt. was formed on 2nd September 1946 and Dr.Rajendra Prasad was assigned Food and Agriculture portfolio.

He was unanimously elected Chairman of Constituent Assembly against his wishes. He wrote that "with faith in God, I devoted myself to the new task". On November 11, 1947, he became the President of Congress for the third time.

At one place, Dr. Rajendra Prasad wrote, "The English Language is so elastic to limitless interpretations". In another place, he opined, "In a country where people profess so many religions and speak different languages, peace and mutual regard can never prevail without unity. Otherwise, one of the communities will suppress and subjugate the other".

He wrote that we should have faith in truth and justice and adopt the creed of non-violence forever. When we have truth and genuine courage and not fear or cowardice, our success is absolutely certain.

On January 26, 1950, Dr. Rajendra Prasad was elected the first President of Republic of India. During his tenure as President of India, he had serious differences with Pandit Jawaharlal Nehru over the Hindu Code Bill. He served the nation as President for 12 years. He relinquished the office of the President on May 14th 1962. Thereafter, he lived in Bihar till his death on February 28th, 1963.

Rajendra Smriti Sangrahalaya in Patna is dedicated to him. He was awarded Country's highest civilian award **"Bharat Ratna".** Dr Rajendra Prasad had two sons; the eldest is Mrityunjay.

Lal Bahadur Shastri

Azadi Ki tarikh lilkhi gaeyi jis dam
Zikr us mein jali Lal Bahadur Ka rahega
Ye nam liya jaega izzat se hamesha
Jhuk Jaenge sir husne aquidat se hamesha

—Padmashree Syed Ahmedullah Qadri

In honesty, simplicity, dedication and devotion, Lal Bahadur Shastri has no parallel. This great man was born on October 2, 1904 at Mughal Sarai, District Ramnagar in Uttar Pradesh in 'Kayastha Srivastava' family.

His father Sharda Prasad was a teacher in a school at Allahabad. His mother Ram Dulari Devi was a very religious lady. She knew Hindi, Urdu, Bengali and English languages.

He lost his father in 1906, when Lal Bahadur Shastri was one and a half year old. His maternal grand-father, Hazari Lal brought-up Lal Bahadur Shastri and his two sisters. With the affection of Hazari Lal, the young Lal Bahadur did not feel the absence of his father. His mother, right from his childhood, taught him good values of life.

After the demise of Hazari Lal, Lal Bahadur Shastri was sent to his aunt's place in Banaras. In Banaras, he was admitted in Harishchandra High School. Self respect and courage were the two virtues that were deeply rooted in his mind. He decided to drop his caste-derived surname Verma (which is the surname of the Kayasth families).

English and History were his favourite subjects in school. Teachers in the school liked him for his simplicity and hard work. One of his teachers Nishkameshwara Misra sowed the seeds of national feelings in Lal Bahadur's mind.

Lal Bahadur studied in Harishchandra High School upto the age of 17 years. Right from childhood, he was influenced by Bal Gangadhar Tilak's slogan *"Swarajya Hamara Janam Sidh Adhikar Hai"*. He was also influenced by Gandhiji's ideas and had heard a lot about him. The speeches of the freedom fighters made him believe that service to motherland is more important than any other matter.

It was customary in the pre-independence era, in majority of the Kayasth families that children receive education in Persian and Urdu languages because these were the official languages at that time. Therefore, Lal Bahadur began his education at the age of four; a *Maulvi* (a Muslim cleric) was appointed to teach him.

When he was studying 10th standard, he took part in first *"Satyagraha"*. He was arrested at the age of 17 years. Later, on the advice of Dr. Bhagwan Das, he joined Kashi Vidyapeeth. In the year 1925, he obtained the degree of "Shastri" from Kashi Vidyapeeth by scoring good marks in English, Hindi and Philosophy. Later, he associated himself with Lok Sevak Mandal.

On May 16, 1927, Lal Bahadur Shastri married Lal Mani Devi, who later came to be known as Lalita Devi. After the marriage, Lal Bahadur Shastri went to Allahabad and joined 'Servants of India Society'.

Lal Bahadur Shastri became the Secretary of District Congress Committee of Allahabad in the year 1930 and continued till 1936. He also became the member of Allahabad Municipality.

Shastriji was arrested and kept in Malka Jail in the suburbs of Allahabad where he used to read books of reputed authors and translated Madame Curie's (a famous scientist) biography in Hindi. He was again arrested in 1932 and was kept in Faizabad jail.

It is a fact that Lalita Devi, wife of Shastriji also participated in many boycott movements with Kamala Nehru and Vijay Laxmi Pandit.

In 1936, Shastriji was elected from Allahabad constituency and became MLA of Uttar Pradesh Legislature. He went to jail several times and was in various jails, such as, Naini Jail etc. Shastriji spent about 12 years in jail.

On an occasion, Shastriji was released on unconditional parole for 15 days to see his ailing daughter. However, his daughter passed away before he reached home. He performed her last rites and after sometime, he went back to jail. The family members insisted that he should stay till the parole period is over. He replied that the parole was given to see his daughter; she has been taken away from us. He returned before the expiry of the parole period. The prison officials were also surprised that Shastriji was very honest when they saw him in jail before the expiry of parole period.

During all these days, when Shastriji was in jail, he was passing through serious financial crisis, his children could not go to school as it was not possible to pay their fees. Lalita Shastri was facing problems to provide even two time meals to children. She started cooking "Bhauri". This is a sort of "Bati" eaten with salt and onion. When his Muslim neighbours came to know about it, they arranged for the supply of ration against the wishes of Lalita Shastri and requested her to accept a small contribution against her outstanding dedication and sacrifice toward the nation.

It is an accepted fact that Lal Bahadur Shastri was known for his capabilities of meeting people and winning their hearts.

Pandit Govind Vallabh Panth when he became Chief Minister of Uttar Pradesh, asked Lal Bahadur Shastri to take over the administration of Uttar Pradesh. Later, after Independence, Shastriji was made Minister of Police and Transport.

After winning Lok Sabha seat in 1952, Shastriji was appointed Minister of Railways and Transport in Central Cabinet. He introduced many reforms in Railways. When a rail accident occurred at Jadcherla in Mahaboobnagar of Telangana State, Lal Bahadur Shastri resigned the post accepting the moral responsibility of the accident.

In 1957, he won Lok Sabha election from Allahabad and was made Minister of Transport and Communication in the Central Cabinet. Later, he was made Home Minister after the demise of Shri Govind Vallabh Panth in 1961. His tenure as Home Minister was full of challenges including Chinese Aggression. Under the Kamaraj Plan, he resigned in 1963. However, in 1964 he was appointed Minister without portfolio.

Pandit Jawaharlal Nehru passed away on 27th May 1964. On June 9, 1964, Shastriji was sworn in as the second Prime Minster of India. He was concerned about the development of Farmers and the Military forces. Thus, he raised the famous slogan "Jai Jawan – Jai Kisan".

Shastriji was keen to have good relations with Pakistan but it was all in vain. Due to anti-Indian activities, in the beginning of 1965, Shaikh Abdullah was kept under surveillance in a house in Otacamund.

In September 1965, Pakistan invaded India at Chamb area of Kahsmir. Thereafter, Lal Bahadur Shastri gave full powers and freedom to army not only to counter attack Pakistan but to move freely inside Pakistan.

After the intervention of many leading countries and UNO India and Pakistan agreed for ceasefire and on September 23rd 1965 both the countries declared ceasefire on the advice of UNO.

On 10th of January, 1966, Shastriji had a serious Myocardial attack in Tashkent where he passed away within few minutes. The entire nation went in grief, some suspected a foul play. The mystery still exists. Shastriji's sudden death led to the persistent conspiracy that he was poisoned, dark blue spots on the body was the cause of raising doubts. His body was brought from Tashkent (Soviet Union). The family was grief stricken. His mother, Ram Dulari Devi and wife, Lalita Shastri were in deep sorrow and grief. The entire nation joined the farewell. Leaders from world over paid tributes to the great man. He was cremated at Vijay Ghat in New Delhi, where a memorial was built.

He was a simple man and lived a simple life. He was honest, sincere and devoted to the cause. He proved himself worthy of a real politician, minister and above all, Prime Minister of India.

Many memorials, stadia, Bhavans, Institutes and Libraries etc. were established in his memory.

In 2005, Government of India created a chair in his honour in the field of Democracy and Governance at Delhi University.

He continued the policies of non-alignment and socialism. He tried to make administration clean and effective. He was of the view that corruption in any form is a crime. He was the follower of Gandhian values and simplicity. He never mixed religion with politics. He was a great patriot, freedom fighter and above all, a remarkable man. He will be remembered with respect by Indian nation for decades to come.

He was of the view that education is an important tool for bringing about a change in social life. Education of girls is as important as the education of boys. The girls should have equal opportunities to learn and qualify.

He was conferred **"Bharat Ratna"** the highest civilian award posthumously by Government of India for the services he rendered for the nation. Shastriji gave India a sense of sincerity and comfort. His style of working with trust and confidence of nation is the guiding principle for the younger generation. His son, Hari Krishna (who is no more) and other sons Anil, Sunil and Ashok also joined politics.

Shastriji's memorial was also constructed at Tashkent (Russia).

Thus, it can be said that - *Hai qaul amal terah hamesha se ham ahang*
kirdar hai terah teri, guftar se hamrang
Shohrat se nah taqat se nah daulat se tujhe kam.
Bas quamki kidmat se gharaz hai sahar wo sham

Padma Shree Syed Ahmed Ullah Qadri

Munshi Prem Chand

Dhanpat Rai Srivastav – popularly known as Munshi Prem Chand was born on 31st July 1880, in Lamabi near Varanasi. He belonged to the Kayasth family. His fore-fathers were holding small lands. His grandfather was a *Patwari* (Village Chief) and his father, Ajaib Rai was serving Postal Department. His mother was Anandi Devi. He was the fourth child of his parents. The first two were girls. They died at an early age; the third was his elder sister, Suggi.

Prem Chand was a man of average height; lean body, lovely oblong face, big and beautiful eyes. He used to put on white turban, collarless jacket and white *pyjama* and *kurta.*

Though his parents named him Dhanpat Rai, his uncle, who was a big landlord named him Nawab Rai. Later, Prem Chand chose this as his pen name.

Prem Chand started going to school at the age of seven years, but very soon his mother passed away, when he was eight years old. He learnt Persian and Urdu from a Maulvi. Later, he studied at Queen's College in Banaras.

In 1895, he married at the age of 15 while he was studying in 9th standard. His wife was from a rich landlord's family. After passing matriculation examination, he sought admission in Hindu College. Subsequently, he discontinued his studies. He got a job of a teacher in a private school and was tutoring students privately. Later, he got a job as a teacher in Government school. His first novel was *"Asrar-e-Ma'abid'* which expresses the corruption among temple priests.

He was posted at Kanpur in 1905. He stayed at Kanpur from 1905 to 1909. During this period, his wife left for her father's place and never returned nor Prem Chand made any attempt to bring her back. In 1906, Prem Chand married a widow child by name Shiv Rani Devi.

In 1907, he wrote his second novel *"Hamkhurma-o-Hamsawab"*. In the same year, he published *"Roothi Rani", Soz-e-Watan"*.

Soz-e-Watan was published in 1909 under the pen name Nawab Rai. *Soz-e-Watan* was based on political stories, such as, division of Bengal "Gram Dal" of the Congress. Police started searching for the author. Prem Chand was called by the Collector of the District and enquired about each and every story written in the book. Prem Chand was told that Nawab Rai wrote against the Government and therefore, he has to hand over all the copies of *Soz-e-Watan* to the Government. By then three 'hundred copies were sold out and the remaining seven hundred copies were handed over to the Government which were later burnt.

Prem Chand passed intermediate examination in 1910 with English, Persian and History, as subjects.

His short stories were published in *"Zamana"* (Kanpur), *"Hamdard"* (Delhi) and *"Adeeb"* (Allahabad).

He wrote *"Jalwa-e-Asar"* in 1916, which was his last book under his pen name, Nawab Rai. After this, he started writing under the name Prem Chand.

The outstanding features of Prem Chand's short stories or *"Afsane"* are patriotism, greatness and glory of nation. Secondly, these stories depict village life and natural behaviour of human beings.

His novels depict the problems of the poor and the middle-class. His main aim was to highlight national and social issues. He wrote extensively about them. In addition to this, he wrote about Feudal System, prostitution, poverty, India's Freedom Struggle and wide range of then prevailing issues.

Urdu novels of Prem Chand are: *Israr-e-ma'abid, Ham-Khurma-o-Hamsawab, Soz-e-watan, Jalwa-e-Asar" Gosha-e-Afiyat, Bazar-e-Husn, Nirmala, Bewa, Chaugan-e-Hasti, Parad-i-Majaz, Gowdaan, Maidan-e-Amal and Karmabhoomi* are worth mentioning among his notable works. He also published a short novel "*Krishna*" in 1907.

After obtaining B.A. degree in 1919, Prem Chand was promoted as Deputy Inspector of Schools. He attended the meetings of Gandhiji who asked people to resign from Government jobs. Prem Chand decided to quit the Government service. Subsequently, he focused on literary work, which was the only source of income to him.

After leaving Government job, he diverted most of his time towards Hindi literature. He started writing editorials for *'Maryada'* (1923), *'Madhuri'* (1928), *'Hans'* (1933), 'Jagaran' (1933).

He had a limited income from Urdu writings. In one of his letters, he wrote that "now I am trying to write in Hindi. It is not possible to maintain myself by writing in Urdu. It appears that I will spend my life in writing in Hindi as late Bal Mukund Gupt". He questioned himself, has any Hindu is benefited in writing in Urdu, how can I ?

Thus in the history of Hindi literature, a glorious period was started in Hindi novels especially in social customs.

His Hindi novels, such as *'Prema'* was his first novel. *"Seva Sadan' (Bazaar-e-Husn), 'Prem Ashram', 'Nirmala'* (1923) *'Rang Bhoomi'* (1928), *'Gowdaan'* etc. earned him substantial money.

His short stories in Hindi also became popular among the masses. Several of them were published in different magazines and in the form of books *'Man Sarovar'*. Some of the popular stories are *'Kafan', "Gupt Daan', 'Shatranj-ke-Khiladi', 'Beti ka Daan', 'Balidaan'. 'Saut', 'Bade Bhai Sab'* etc.

Prem Chand was the follower of Swami Vivekananda.

While expressing his views about Prem Chand, Dr. Syed Mohiuddin Qadri Zore wrote that Prem Chand was a renowned Urdu writer. He is among the rare patrons of Urdu literature. His efforts made Urdu, the second largest language of the world.

According to Prof. Al-e-Ahmed Suroor, "Prem Chand was not only a short story writer but a great novelist as well". His outstanding novels are *Bazaar-e-Husn, Maidan-e-Amal, Nirmala, Gowdaan* etc. He is of the view that *Chaugan-e-Hasti* is the best Urdu novel which was published in 1924.

Prem Chand went to Bombay in 1934 and tried his luck in Hindi films. He wrote a script for a film *'Mazdoor'* which was released but was banned later. He came back from Bombay in 1935. Besides short stories, novels and scripts he wrote some plays, as well, such as, *'Sangram', 'Karbala', 'Roohani Shadi'* etc. some of the theatre companies staged his plays and short stories, such as, *'Kafan'* etc. Prem Chand also wrote the biography of *'Saadi'*.

Films were made based on his short stories, such as, *'Kafan'* (Telugu) *'Shatranj-ke-Khiladi'* in Hindi etc.

He presided over the Conference of Progressive Writers in 1935.

Prem Chand passed away on October 8th, 1936 at the age of 56.

Prem Chand was a man of etiquette and manners. He was a very simple person. Eventhough, he gained fame and became India's renowned and outstanding Urdu writer, literary figure and novelist, but he never had any proud which is a universally accepted fact.

Prem Chand had two sons born to Shiv Rani Devi. The first one was Sripat Rai who was born in 1919 in Gorakhpur and second Amrit Rai was born in Kanpur in 1922. Prem Chand also had a daughter. However, another son who was also born in Gorakhpur died of chicken pox at the young age.

In short, he wrote more than 12 novels, about 250 short stories and several essays.

Neither Prem Chand hurt any one with his words nor with his pen. He was a generous and a kind-hearted person. Once, when his wife gave him money to purchase clothes for himself, he distributed it among his press employees.

'Prem Sog' was the first book written on him after his death by Mohammad Husamuddin Khan Ghori. This book gives a complete picture of Prem Chand. Thereafter, voluminous work has been done on Prem Chand and several volumes had written on him. Many awards were instituted in the memory of Prem Chand.

Shiv Rani Devi was Prem Chand's second wife. Before her marriage, she had the working knowledge of Hindi but after her marriage, she gained proficiency in this language. Subsequently, she became a famous short story writer. Her first collection of stories *'Nari Hriday'* based on 16 stories and the second is *'Sindoor ki Rekha'*. She not only contributed to literature along with Prem Chand but took active role in politics. She was sent to jail. She took active role in literary and national activities after the death of Prem Chand. Her works have been translated and published in different languages.

It can, therefore, be concluded that Prem Chand is the renowned novelist, India has ever produced.

Maha Devi Verma

Maha Devi Verma was a distinguished Hindi Poetess of the 20th Century. She belonged to Kayasth family of eminent lawyers. She was born in Farrukhabad on 26th March 1907 (1964 Saraswat). Her father's name was Govind Pershad Verma and her mother's name was Hema Rani Devi. Hema Rani Devi also occasionally wrote poems. Her father was the Head master in a school in Bhagalpur. Maha Devi Verma was brought up in this culture and atmosphere from childhood.

She had her early education till 6th standard in Bhagalpur. She was married at the age of eleven. Her husband, Dr. Swaroop Narayan Verma was the resident of Buroli. Her father-in-law was against girl's education. Maha Devi Verma stood first in the middle standard. She studied in Crosthwaite Girls College in Allahabad. She also passed B.A. examination in 1929. Later, she passed M.A. in Sanskrit from Prayag University, Allahabad, in first division in 1933.

Her grandfather desired that she should become a scholar. In fact, her mother was very fluent in Hindi and Sanskrit languages. It was her mother who inspired her to write poems and thus developed interest in literature.

She wrote both in poetry and prose. She also wrote articles. Her prose writings are no less important than poetry. In her articles, she has dealt with in detail about woman's life. Maha Devi and Sumitra used to send poems to weekly magazine for publication, while they were in School. Sumitra was senior to Maha Devi in the school. Later, Maha Devi Verma became the Principal of the Prayag Mahila Vidyapeeth and then became the Chancellor.

Some of the famous literacy works of Maha Devi Verma are:

'Mere Bachpan ke Din', *'Gilla'*, *'Neehar'* (1930), *'Rashmi'* (1932), *'Neeraja'* (1934), *'Sandhya Geet'* (1936), *'Deep Shika'* (1942), *'Yama'* *'Path ke Sathi'*, *'Maha Devi ka Vivechanatmak Gadya'*, *'Smiriti ki Rekhayen'* (1942), *Shrankhla ki Kadigan'*, *'Shanda'* etc. and *'Agni Rekha'* (1990) published after her death.

It is a fact that Maha Devi is one of the four major poets of Chayawad School of Hindi Literature, a period of romanticism in modern Hindi language from 1914-1938. The others are Sumitra Nandan Pant, Jaya Krishna Prasad and Surya Kanth Tripathi 'Nirala'. However, her status was altogether different from the other writers of Chayawad.

Her contribution to Hindi literature is not only valuable but also inestimable. She started writing in 'Khadi Boli' and later wrote in 'Braj Bhasha'.

She worked tirelessly for the education of women and their economic uplift. She constructed a house in 1936 in Ramgarh about 25 km. from Nainital and named it 'Meera Mandir'. Today, this bungalow is known as 'Maha Devi Sahitya Sangrahlaya'. She is considered to be a social worker for her contribution in various social works.

She was closely associated with a large number of writers and others, such as, Suryakanth Tripathi, 'Nirala', Gopi Kishan, Gopaish, Sumitra Nandan Pant, Ganga Pershad Pandey, his son, Ramji Pandey, did a great service to Maha Devi Verma during her last days.

A brief script below provides the dates of important events in the life of Maha Devi Verma. This speaks volumes of her contributions and activities during her life time.

Maha Devi Verma – A Brief Script

1907	-	Born on a Holi Day in Farukhabad, Uttar Pradesh.
1912	-	Commencement of education at Indore.
1916	-	Got married – Education discontinued.
1919	-	Recommencement of education, Crosthwaite Girls' College, Prayag.
1921	-	Stood first in the entire state in middle school examination, was granted State Scholarship, met Mahatma Gandhi.
1925	-	Stood first at the Entrance Examination and received Scholarship again.
1927	-	Passed Intermediate examination in first division - received Scholarship.
1929	-	Passed B.A. examination. Attempted to become Boudh Bhikshuni. Her inclination toward social work ommenced after meeting Mahatma Gandhi in Takula (Nainital). On the motivation of Gandhiji, she started educational activities and work.
1930	-	She stayed in Nainital for a long period due to ill health. First All India Poetess gathering was inaugurated in Prayag.
1932	-	Obtained M.A. in Sanskrit from Prayag University (Allahabad University). On the motivation of Gandhi ji, she postponed the foreign visit for higher education, propagation of women's education through Hindi. Establishment of Mahila Vidyapeeth Maha Vidyalaya and took the responsibility as the Vice-Chancellor of the Vidyapeeth. Launched monthly magazine *"Chand"*.

1933 - Came in close contact with Dr. Rabindranath Tagore in Prayag. Organised first Meera Jayanti.

1934 - Awarded Sakseriya Prize for her poetic collection *Neeraja'*.

1935 - Attended the welcome ceremony of the Japanese Poet Naguchi, as a Poetess in Calcutta. She was the guest of Dr. Rabindranath Tagore in Shantiniketan.

1936 - Her poetry collection – 'Yama' published in 1936 received Gyanpeeth Award. This is one of the highest Indian Literary Award.

1937 - Inauguration of Meera Mandir in Ramgarh, Nainital.

1939 - Second Pilgrimage to Badr-Kedar on foot.

1941 - Publication of 'Budh Ank' of Vishwawani.

1942 - Was awarded *'Dwedi Padak'* for *'Smriti ki Rehkayen'*. Helped secretly in the August Kranti Movement.

1943 - Received 'Mangla Prasad' *Puraskar* and 'Bharat Bharti' Award.

1944 - Establishment of *'Sahityakar Sansad'*.

1949 - Under the auspices of *'Sahityakar Sansad'* in Prayag, the Akhil Bharatiya Writers' Conference was organized.

1951 - Laying down of foundation stone of the Vani Mandir in Sahityakar Sansad Bhavan by Dr. Rajendra Prasad First President of India. Prasad Parv was organized.

1952 - Nominated member of the Uttar Pradesh Vidhan Parishad. Led the delegation of the Hindi *Lekhak Mandal* to South India. Struggle for the amendment to Co-operative Rules with the Central Government.

1954 - Was nominated as Member of Sahitya Academy, New Delhi.

1955 - Publication of *'Sahityakar'* monthly under the auspices of Sahityakar Sansad. Sahityakar Inter State Conference was organized at Takula in Nainital. *'Rangwani'* Dramatic organization was established. Difference of opinion with the then Education Minister Maulana Azad on the conference of different languages.

1956 - Was awarded Padma Bhushan by Government of India.

1957 - Struggled with her long illness.

1960 - was appointed Vice-Chancellor of Prayag University (Allahabad University).

1963 - Welcome by President Dr. Radhakrishnan on behalf of Lekhika Sangh – Delhi.

1964 - *'Abhinandan Granth Bhent'* on behalf of Bharatiya Parishad Prayag.

1967 - Maha Devi Sansmaran Granth – Edited by Pant was presented on the occasion of Golden Jubilee celebrations.

1968 - Returned the Padma Bhushan award in protest of policy of Government of India against Hindi language.

1969 - Delivered lecture at Vikram University, Ujjain, was awarded Honorary Doctorate Degree of Vikram University.

1979 - Was the first woman to be awarded 'Sahitya Academy Fellowship'.

1988 - Government of India bestowed on her with Padma Vibhushan, the second highest civilian award.

1991 - Postal Department of Government of India issued Two Rupee Postage Stamp in honour of Maha Devi Verma along with Jaishankar Pershad.

Maha Devi Verma shifted to Allahabad after the demise of her husband Dr. Swaroop Narayan Verma, in1966.

Maha Devi Verma passed away on 11th September 1987 at the age of 80 years.

She lived the life of a Saint.

Dr Shanti Swaroop Bhatnagar

A Scientist of Repute

Dr. Shanti Swaroop Bhatnagar, a Scientist of repute was born on 21st February, 1894, in the then undivided Punjab. He was born in the Kayasth educated elite family. His father, Parmeshwar Sahay Bhatnagar was a graduate from Punjab University. His mother Parvati Devi Bhatnagar was the eldest daughter of Praye Lal who was a distinguished engineer. His father, Parmesri Sahai Bhatnagar passed away when Shanti Swaroop Bhatnagar was 8 months old. His father, lost the share of his property because of his refusal to follow the traditions of the family. However, he continued to serve society. When he passed away, he left his wife and children in dire poverty. His maternal grandfather, Rai Bahadur Munshi Manohar Lal Bhatnagar a distinguished engineer, brought him up. He was known for his honesty. Thus, he spent his childhood in his maternal house.

He had his early education in Anglo-Vedic High School. In 1911, he joined Dayal Singh College. He passed his intermediate examination in 1913 from Punjab University. He did his B.Sc. in 1916 from the then Christian College. He obtained his M.Sc. in 1919 in Chemistry. Later, he was awarded D.Sc. in 1921 by London University. His topic of research was "Solubility of bivalent and trivalent Salts of higher fatty acids in oils and their effects on surface tension of Oils". His research guide was Fredrick G. Donnanm.

After completing his D.Sc. in London, he came back to India and joined Banaras Hindu University as Professor of Chemistry.

Later, he joined the University of Punjab as Professor of Physical Chemistry and became the Director of Chemical Laboratories.

He jointly invented a magnetic interference balance called "Bhatnagar-Mathur Balance". He did a major work of improving the procedure for drilling crude oil. A company financed for setting up a Department of Petroleum Research under the guidance of Dr. Bhatnagar. Appreciating his services in innovations, the company increased the financial support and extended the period from 5 – 10 years.

Dr. Bhatnagar in collaboration with Dr. K.N. Mathur wrote the book entitled *"Physical Principles and Application of Magneto Chemistry"*. This book was published and recognized as an outstanding contribution.

Dr. Bhatnagar's interest in literature and poetry comes from his mother's side. His mother's family had a number of poets, such as, Munshi Har Gopal Tufta who got the title of 'Mirza' from 'Mirza Ghalib' the great Urdu and Persian Poet. The family of Dr. Bhatnagar adorned the Mughal Court and was bestowed with the title of *'Khawaja-i-Khawaja'*. Dr. Bhatnagar wrote poems under the title *'Lajwanti'* in Urdu in memory of his wife, which were 'subsequently published.

He wrote a one-act play in Urdu called *'Karamati'* (wonder worker). This was considered to be the best play of the year 1912. The English translation of the play earned him a prize and a medal of Saraswati Stage Society in the year 1912 as the best play of the year. Dr. Bhatnagar himself was a good actor.

Dr. Shanti Swaroop Bhatnagar was appointed as the Director of the Council of Scientific and Industrial Research in 1940 by then he was one of the leading scientists of India. Later, the Council of Scientific and Industrial Research was set up as the autonomous body. The governing body of CSIR approved the proposal mooted by Dr.Bhatnagar to set up five national laboratories viz. - The National Chemical Laboratory, National Physical Laboratory etc.

Dr. Bhatnagar was closely associated with the renowned scientists like Dr. Jehangir Homi Bhabha and Dr. Vikram Sarabhai. He contributed immensely in the development and implementation of Government policies of Science and Technology in the post-independent era. The shining example is the Council of Scientific and Industrial Research (CSIR), which was set up under the Chairmanship of Dr.Bhatnagar.

He established as many as 12 National Laboratories, to name a few: Central Food Processing Technology Institute, National Metallurgical Laboratory, National Chemical Laboratory, National Physical Laboratory etc.

He also served as the Secretary in the Ministry of Education, Government of India, and also in advisory capacity in many organizations.

Dr. Bhatnagar was conferred the Order of the British Empire (OBE) in the year 1936, by the British Government.

He was knighted in the year 1941. He was elected Fellow of Royal Society (FRS) in 1943.

In 1954, he was awarded **'Padma Bhushan'**, the third highest civilian award given by Government of India.

The Council of Scientific and Industrial Research instituted a prestigious award to be given for the notable and outstanding research in the field of Biology, Chemistry, Environmental Science, Engineering, Mathematics, Medicine and Physics in memory of Dr. Bhatnagar. The award is known as **'Dr. Shanti Swaroop Bhatnagar Award**.' This was first awarded in the year 1958.

Dr. Shanti Swaroop Bhatnagar passed away on 1st January, 1955 at the age of 60.

Pandit Jawahar Lal Nehru said"

"I have been associated with many prominent figures, eminent in other ways, but Dr. Bhatnagar was a special combination of many things, added to which was a tremendous energy with enthusiasm to achieve things. The result was he left a record of achievement, which was truly remarkable. I can truly say that but for Dr. Bhatnagar you could not have seen today the chain of National Laboratories".

Dr. Bhatnagar is considered to be the father of National Laboratories in India

References

Primary Sources

Miscellaneous Manuscripts

Daily Diaries of Bansi Raja 1883 – 1896.

Secondary Sources

English Books

Chabbra, Harisharan, *Hyderabad Personalities*, New Publishers, Delhi – 1954,

Khanna, Monica, *Lal Bahadur Shastri, a great son of Mother India,* Farsight Publishers and Distributors, Delhi – 2013.

Leonard, Karen, Isaksen *Social History of an India Caste, the Kayasthhas of Hyderabad,* University of California, Press, California, 1978.

Mudiraj, K.Krishnaswamy, *Pictorial Hyderabad,* two vols. Chandrakanth Press, Hyderabad, 1929, 1934.

Rajendra Prasad, *An Autobiography,* Asian Publishing House, Bombay, 1957.

Raj, Sheela, *Mediaevalism to Modernism,* Popular Prakashan, Bombay, 1997.

Raj, Sheela, *Portrait of an Era, Hyderabad in the Days of Nizams, 1828-1896* – Minerva Press, London, 1990.

Raj, Sheela, *The Religious Tolerance of the Asaf Jahi Kings and Hindu-Muslim Traditions,* Narhari Pershad Charitable Trust, Hyderabad, 2010.

Wikipedia – Encyclopedia.

Urdu Books

Akbar, Jalaluddin, *Hyderabadi- Shuara,* S.A. Graphics, Hyderabad, 2009.

Ghori Husam Uddin Khan Mohammed, *Prem Sog,* Maktaba Ibrahimiya, Hyderabad, 1935.

Qadri Ahmedullah. *A Humble Tribute to Shri Lal Bahadur Shastri.* Rafeeq Press, Hyderabad, 1964.

Qadri Ahmedullah, *Bahadur Naama,* Lutfuddoula Oriental Research Institute, Hyderabad, 1965.

Raj, Sheela, *Diwan-i-Aali*, Narhari Pershad Charitable Trust, Hyderabad, 2008.

Raj, Sheela, *Diwan-i-Mahbub,* Narhari Pershad Charitable Trust, Hyderabad, 2005.

Siddiqui, Mohd. Akbaruddin - *Prem Chand Aur Unki Afsana Nigari*, Office, Anjuman Tilsaneen Osmania, 1945.

Hindi Books

Saxena, Bhaskar Raj, *Hyderabad Nizam Kal Ke Bhakt Kavi 1762 – 1957-A.D.*

Sharma, Kapil *Vishwa-ki-Vygyanic Vibhutiyan.*

Maan Publishers, Hyderabad 2002.

Verma, Shyamla Kant, *Lekhakh Samiksha,* Sanjay Book Centre, Varanasi.

Miscellaneous – Hindi

Maha Devi Varma Jeevan Rekha

Maha Devi Varma Maha Bharat

Journals

Multani, Syed Moizuddin Qadri, *R.R. Saxena,* Subras, August 1991.

Saxena, Mahender Raj, *Deccan-ke-Chand Kayasth Shohra, Subras* January 1940, p. 39.

Index

D

M

N

O

P

Q

R